WINDOWS AZURE® WEB SITES

MW00964436

Windows Azure® Web Sites

James Chambers

wrox™

A Wiley Brand

Windows Azure® Web Sites

Published by
John Wiley & Sons, Inc.
10475 Crosspoint Boulevard
Indianapolis, IN 46256
www.wiley.com

Copyright © 2013 by John Wiley & Sons, Inc., Indianapolis, Indiana
Published simultaneously in Canada

ISBN: 978-1-118-67852-7
ISBN: 978-1-118-67864-0 (ebk)
ISBN: 978-1-118-74979-1 (ebk)

ACQUISITIONS EDITOR
Mary James

SENIOR PROJECT EDITOR
Ami Frank Sullivan

TECHNICAL EDITORS
Bruce Johnson
Cory Fowler

SENIOR PRODUCTION EDITOR
Kathleen Wisor

COPY EDITOR
Luann Rouff

EDITORIAL MANAGER
Mary Beth Wakefield

FREELANCER EDITORIAL MANAGER
Rosemarie Graham

ASSOCIATE DIRECTOR OF MARKETING
David Mayhew

MARKETING MANAGER
Ashley Zurcher

VICE PRESIDENT AND EXECUTIVE GROUP PUBLISHER
Richard Swadley

VICE PRESIDENT AND EXECUTIVE PUBLISHER
Neil Edde

ASSOCIATE PUBLISHER
Jim Minatel

PROOFREADER
Nancy Carrasco

COVER DESIGNER
Ryan Sneed

ABOUT THE AUTHOR

JAMES CHAMBERS is a presenter, long-time blogger, and geek who loves the craft and the tools that he works with. He works on open source projects such as Twitter.Bootstrap.Mvc4 and AngelaSmith and contributes to the docs project for NuGet. He has worked at all three levels of Canadian government, with social and military firms, in food service and insurance, in telecommunication, and even the auto industry. He enjoys mentoring, learning from others and sharing his development experiences at conferences, web camps, user group meetings, and brown bag lunches. You can find him online at http://jameschambers.com or on Twitter as @CanadianJames. He lives in rural Manitoba — the epicenter of software development in Canada — where he and his wife are raising three mancubs and surviving the ownership of a dog and a cat.

ABOUT THE TECHNICAL EDITOR

CORY FOWLER is a Windows Azure Technical Evangelist at Microsoft Corporation. He has been working with Windows Azure since shortly after the beginning of the public beta in 2008, gaining him two consecutive MVP awards for his work in the Windows Azure community before joining Microsoft. Cory has extensive experience in web development spanning from Startup to Enterprise with various Server-side languages, including but not limited to ASP.NET, PHP, Perl/CGI. You can read more about Windows Azure Web Sites on Cory's blog http://blog.syntaxc4.net or follow Cory on Twitter under the handle @SyntaxC4.

ACKNOWLEDGMENTS

THANKS go to my incredible wife, Angie, who is supportive beyond reason, beautiful inside and out, and the perfect mother to our three awesome, inspiring children, Beemer, Pants, and Molly. Thanks to Cory and Bruce who helped make these pages come together, and Ami and Mary for putting up with my "timely" delivery. Though the work on this book has been short, it has been through a rough patch, so thanks to James 1:2-5 for helping me to keep focus. Thanks to my good friends, Edwin and Fred, who are walking through troubling times and showing me what true character is; and thank you to Kevin and Keith who have demonstrated wisdom, grace, and compassion that I can only hope to emulate.

CONTENTS

INTRODUCTION TO THE WINDOWS AZURE BOOK SERIES

It has been fascinating watching the maturation of Windows Azure since its introduction in 2008. When it was announced, Azure was touted as being Microsoft's "new operating system." And at that level, it has not really lived up to its billing. However, if you consider Azure to be a collection of platforms and tools that allow you to cloud-enable your corporation's applications and infrastructure, well, now you're on the right track.

And, as it turns out, a collection of cooperating tools and services is the best way to think of Azure. The different components that comprise Azure become building blocks that allow you to construct an environment to suit your needs. Want to be able to host a simple website? Well, then Azure Web Sites fits the bill. Want to move some of your infrastructure to the cloud while leaving other systems on premise? Azure Virtual Networking gives you the capability to extend your corporate domain to include machines hosted in Azure. Almost without exception, each twist and turn in your infrastructure roadmap can take advantage of the building blocks that make up Windows Azure.

A single book covering everything that encompasses Azure would be huge. And because of the breadth of components in Azure, such a book is likely to contain information that you are not necessarily interested in. For this reason, the Windows Azure series from Wrox takes the same "building block" approach that Azure does. Each book in the series drills deeply into one technology. If you want to learn everything you need to work with a particular technology, then you could not do better than to pick up the book for that topic. But you don't have to dig through 2,000 pages to find the 120 pages that matter to you. Each book stands on its own. You can pick up the books for the topics you are care about and know that's all that you will get. And you can leave the other books until desire or circumstance makes them of interest to you.

So enjoy this book. It will give you the information you need to put Windows Azure to use for you. But as you continue to look to other Azure components to add to your infrastructure, don't forget to check out the other books in the series to see what topics might be helpful. The books in the series are:

- ➤ *Windows Azure and ASP.NET MVC Migration* by Benjamin Perkins, Senior Support Escalation Engineer, Microsoft

- ➤ *Windows Azure Mobile Services* by Bruce Johnson, MVP, Partner, ObjectSharp Consulting

- ➤ *Windows Azure Web Sites* by James Chambers, Product & Community Development Manager, LogiSense

➤ *Windows Azure Data Storage* by Simon Hart, Software Architect, Microsoft

➤ *Windows Azure Hybrid Cloud* by Danny Garber, Windows Azure Solution Architect, Microsoft; Jamal Malik, Business Solution Architect; and Adam Fazio, Solution Architect, Microsoft

Each one of these books was written with the same thought in mind: to provide deep knowledge of that one topic. As you go further into Azure, you can pick and choose what makes sense for you from the other books that are available. Constructing your knowledge using these books is like building blocks, which is just in the same manner that Azure was designed.

Bruce Johnson
Azure Series Book Editor

INTRODUCTION TO *WINDOWS AZURE WEB SITES*

I'll make a quick observation on the past experiences of many web developers who tried to put a website on "the cloud" — it really wasn't very good. Most of us didn't know where to start, and even if you were very familiar with the steps, you needed a careful and calculated approach to configure and move your site into the sky. Missteps cost hours and there was little support or collective knowledge to help resolve issues.

Throw all that away. If you have been burned in a similar scenario, you can forget about those experiences; you are going to be pleasantly surprised with the offering of Windows Azure Web Sites. A point-and-click interface gives you the power to scale your site to support tens of thousands of users, with publishing simplified to the point of one-button deployment. You can wire different configurations and transformations into your website and automate the process of moving your application into staging and production environments with tools you likely already know.

The keen reader may have already noticed the spelling of "Web Sites" versus "website." While "website" is the generally accepted spelling for the application that lives on the other end of a URL, the product name is officially "Windows Azure Web Sites." Throughout the book, "Web Sites" or even WAWS refers to the product proper.

WHO THIS BOOK IS FOR

The content of this book is well suited to developers using the .NET Framework to build web applications, to folks who are building applications on PHP or Node.js, and to programmers and managers who are interested in learning more about how to deploy and manage websites in the cloud. This is not a book about learning to program or building a site, but about learning how to get your site onto the Internet using the features of Windows Azure Web Sites.

Maybe you're a .NET developer but you want to learn more about alternative development platforms and where they fit in Azure. Or, perhaps you're from a different technology stack and you want to equip yourself with information on Azure, and how you could use it in your context. Chapters 5 and 7 will be most relevant to you, exploring a PHP site from an open-source forum project and later using the Azure Management Portal to grow your site.

If you have general familiarity with Windows Azure and are already comfortable working in the Azure Management Portal, you might be most interested in using the first few chapters as a reference when required and jumping straight to Chapter 4, which introduces management of WAWS from the console. Chapters 7 and 8 discuss configuring, monitoring, and scaling your site, and walk you through a sample deployment.

WHAT THIS BOOK COVERS

This book provides a walk-through of the Windows Azure Web Sites features that matter to developers and explains how they can be leveraged, as illustrated by an accompanying project. Readers can expect to walk away with an understanding of the supported technologies, site deployment and management tools, and how to monitor and scale their application. Covered in the book and its accompanying materials are the following:

- ➤ Creation, deployment, and scaling of applications
- ➤ Supported project types and technologies
- ➤ Source control integration and release management
- ➤ A detailed walk-through of an application, including prepping it and moving it to the cloud using techniques and features discussed throughout the book

HOW THIS BOOK IS STRUCTURED

If you have built and deployed a website to any server, then you likely already know all the basics needed to build and deploy a website to the cloud. Windows Azure Web Sites has its own nuances and differences from what some would consider traditional deployment. This book is arranged in such a way that regardless of your background, if you are familiar with web development you should gain a better understanding of the process in the context of Windows Azure Web Sites.

The culmination of what you learn in the early chapters arrives in Chapter 8, where you will take a pre-built ASP.NET MVC application and prepare to move it to the cloud.

Chapter 1: Introduction to Windows Azure and Fundamental Concepts

Windows Azure Web Sites provide a very low-friction starting point for new and low-volume websites, as well as a clean way to scale up your application as its popularity and resource demands grow. You will work through several starting points to warm up and then take a sample application — something comparable to a real-world application that would be deployed to physical hardware — and see what it takes to bring it to the cloud and manage it while it's there.

Chapter 2: Moving an Application to the Cloud

Working from a simple sample application you'll be introduced to the bare essentials of moving an IIS-based deployment to the cloud. There are a number of tools that allow direct publishing, enabling you to selectively move files or publish your entire site; these are the ones that are most like the familiar "xcopy" deployment.

Chapter 3: Managing Deployments via Source Control

The websites you're building are likely much more than single, static pages. Many developers work on teams with a central code repository, but even if they're working alone most developers have adopted source control as part of their toolkit. In this chapter you will become familiar with source control deployments in the context of Windows Azure Web Sites and learn how deployments can be created from various source control servers, largely automated and initiated simply by checking your code in.

Chapter 4: Managing Windows Azure Web Sites from the Console

This chapter provides an overview of the command-line tools available for cross-platform management of your Windows Azure account. While not limited to Web Sites, the console enables you to perform most actions you can carry out in the portal from your local machine. Understanding the pieces of WAWS that can be scripted is critical to automating your build process and incorporating WAWS as part of a continuous deployment project.

Chapter 5: Working with Other Flavors of Windows Azure Web Sites

Not all websites need to be built on ASP.NET, and not all sites have to be built from scratch. Here you'll be introduced to the alternative options for development languages and some of the kick-start apps developers can use as a base for their site. Specifically, you'll have the opportunity to walk through creating, altering, and deploying a PHP site using tools native to the Azure developer.

Chapter 6: Using Peripheral Features with Windows Azure Web Sites

Building a website on Windows Azure Web Sites means that you can also easily leverage other assets you've built on Azure. In this chapter you use the Management Portal to link those resources to your website and learn how to share access to those resources with others.

Chapter 7: Scaling, Configuring, and Monitoring Your Site

As a site grows in popularity it often requires additional resources to accommodate the growth, and good business dictates that you maximize the resources you have to keep your expenses in check. Developers also have to consider branding and how users access a site. This chapter demonstrates how to use the Management Portal to monitor website growth, how to use custom domains, and finally how to scale when the time is right.

Chapter 8: Deploying and Configuring a Cloud Application

To close the book, you'll explore a pre-built reference application, examining the key components of the application and how these pieces interact. You'll learn to work with connection strings and application settings and deploy an application using GitHub.

WHAT YOU NEED TO USE THIS BOOK

All the software used in this book to build, deploy, and maintain your website is either free or free for trial use. Much of it can be downloaded from Microsoft's various web properties.

The easiest way to get the tooling for the .NET projects is to visit http://asp.net/mvc and use the Web Platform Installer. You can also use the links in the Management Portal to get some of the software running locally. You'll want to install the following:

➤ **Visual Studio 2012** — Web, Professional, or Ultimate trial versions are OK to work with in this book. Be sure to get the latest updates to VS and NuGet (you'll be prompted when you run the IDE).

➤ **Azure SDK 2.0** — This updates tooling in VS and enables the latest features to manage your site remotely.

➤ **WebMatrix 3** — Completely Azure-enabled and tied to your subscription, this is an alternate development environment for those who don't require the beefy install of Visual Studio 2012.

You'll also get a chance to try out some online services and see how they integrate or can coexist with your development efforts. To do this, you should create an account with the following properties if you don't already have one:

➤ http://www.windowsazure.com

➤ http://www.github.com

➤ http://www.bitbucket.com

➤ http://www.dropbox.com

➤ http://tfs.visualstudio.com

➤ http://www.codeplex.com

CONVENTIONS

To help you get the most from the text and keep track of what's happening, we've used a number of conventions throughout the book.

> **NOTE** *Notes, warnings, tips, hints, tricks, and asides to the current discussion are offset and placed in italics like this.*

As for styles in the text:

➤ We *highlight* new terms and important words when we introduce them.

➤ We show keyboard strokes like this: Ctrl+A.

➤ We show filenames, URLs, and code within the text like so: `persistence.properties`.

We present code in one of two ways:

```
We use a monofont type with no highlighting for most code examples.
```

We use bold to highlight code of particular importance.

SOURCE CODE

As you work through the examples in this book, you may choose either to type in all the code manually or to use the source code files that accompany the book. All the source code used in this book is available for download at `http://www.wrox.com`. If there are any files to be downloaded to work through a chapter, the filenames and/or project names will be noted in a list at the beginning of the chapter. Once at the site, simply locate the book's title (either by using the Search box or by using one of the title lists) and click the Download Code link on the book's detail page to obtain all the source code for the book.

> **NOTE** *Because many books have similar titles, you may find it easiest to search by ISBN; this book's ISBN is 978-1-118-67864-0 (ePDF) or 978-1-118-74979-1 (ePub).*

Once you download the code, just decompress it with your favorite compression tool. Alternately, you can go to the main Wrox code download page at `www.wrox.com/dynamic/books/download.aspx` to see the code available for this book and all other Wrox books.

ERRATA

We make every effort to ensure that there are no errors in the text or in the code. However, no one is perfect, and mistakes do occur. If you find an error in one of our books, such as a spelling mistake or a faulty piece of code, we would be very grateful for your feedback. By sending in errata you may save another reader hours of frustration and at the same time you will be helping us provide even higher quality information.

To find the errata page for this book, go to http://www.wrox.com and locate the title using the Search box or one of the title lists. Then, on the book details page, click the Book Errata link. On this page you can view all errata that has been submitted for this book and posted by Wrox editors. A complete book list, including links to each book's errata, is also available at www.wrox.com/misc-pages/booklist.shtml.

If you don't spot "your" error on the Book Errata page, go to www.wrox.com/contact/techsupport.shtml and complete the form there to send us the error you have found. We'll check the information and, if appropriate, post a message to the book's errata page and fix the problem in subsequent editions of the book.

P2P.WROX.COM

For author and peer discussion, join the P2P forums at p2p.wrox.com. The forums are a web-based system for you to post messages relating to Wrox books and related technologies and interact with other readers and technology users. The forums offer a subscription feature to e-mail you topics of interest of your choosing when new posts are made to the forums. Wrox authors, editors, other industry experts, and your fellow readers are present on these forums.

At http://p2p.wrox.com you will find a number of different forums that will help you not only as you read this book, but also as you develop your own applications. To join the forums, just follow these steps:

1. Go to http://p2p.wrox.com and click the Register link.

2. Read the terms of use and click Agree.

3. Complete the required information to join as well as any optional information you wish to provide and click Submit.

4. You will receive an e-mail with information describing how to verify your account and complete the joining process.

NOTE *You can read messages in the forums without joining P2P but in order to post your own messages, you must join.*

Once you join, you can post new messages and respond to messages other users post. You can read messages at any time on the web. If you would like to have new messages from a particular forum e-mailed to you, click the Subscribe to this Forum icon by the forum name in the forum listing.

For more information about how to use the Wrox P2P, be sure to read the P2P FAQs for answers to questions about how the forum software works as well as many common questions specific to P2P and Wrox books. To read the FAQs, click the FAQ link on any P2P page.

1

Introduction to Windows Azure and Fundamental Concepts

IN THIS CHAPTER:

➤ The role of Windows Azure Web Sites and how it may find a place in your workflow

➤ An introduction to the Windows Azure Management Portal in the context of a website developer

➤ The basics of creating a simple site

➤ How application state management differs from IIS

➤ Setting deployment credentials

References to "the cloud" seem to be everywhere. Targeted developer advertisements, corporate messaging, and even consumer marketing have all been invaded by this new use of a common word. You can't drive by a bank of city billboards or walk down the corridor of an airport terminal without seeing mention of cloud computing in some form. Heck, by the end of this book, "cloud" won't even sound like a real word anymore!

Indeed, at this point in the Internet's history, it's almost impossible to have any kind of Internet presence without being "in" the cloud, even if you were unaware of it. The most popular mail services have all been cloud-based for some time, as have music and movie services. Nearly every smartphone vendor offers some kind of cloud feature set that it tries to leverage as a marketing point to distinguish itself from the competition. Even the latest versions of document- and photo-editing software have built-in cloud features, or are themselves built on top of the cloud fabric. It's not surprising that the same can be said about our operating systems as well.

By now you have likely wrestled through some of what it means to be "in" the cloud — perhaps you've even tried to host an application or two on a cloud server. However, neither marketing blurbs from vendors nor water cooler talk about the "cloud" among developers will answer all your questions. This book will guide you, as a web developer, from the initial steps of creating a website in the cloud to some of the more advanced operations you will need to manage a successful application. However, before diving into what the cloud means to the solution you're creating, first take a moment to understand what the cloud is not, then circle back to what the cloud is and how it can work for you. I'll keep this short, and I'll make no attempt to sugar coat it. The cloud is not right for all scenarios. It isn't an assurance that your app will scale without issue, nor does it fix any bugs. It should not be viewed as the go-to solution when, for myriad other reasons, you're having trouble keeping your app up to the expectations of your users. It does not automatically make your app more performant, more popular, or more profitable.

"Great," you're thinking, "now what?"

Don't worry. The cloud still offers quite a few benefits to kick around, especially as they relate to web developers. For example, one more thing the cloud doesn't do is throw away everything you've learned about development to date! Recent advancements in the developer experience have made it much easier to get started. It's relatively simple to hook into a variety of continuous integration systems, and deployment is straightforward. You can tie into other cloud features such as storage, content distribution networks, identity, and caching without having to overhaul your app, and the flexibility to scale is also possible. You don't have to perform any significant amount of server admin to get a website turned on, and you can start applying your skills as a .NET web developer by simply clicking File ➪ New Project.

To paint a picture: At this point you're a web developer who has an idea about what the cloud is and what it's not. The following sections dive deeper to give a more expansive, detailed picture of how Windows Azure Web Sites will fit into your toolkit.

NOTE *This first chapter covers the Windows Azure Portal as it relates to managing Windows Azure Web Sites. If you are already comfortable within the portal, you may wish to move on to Chapter 2, which introduces the sample application that serves as the focus of this book. If you would like a refresher on the portal, or you haven't worked with a recent version of it, this chapter is a good place to start.*

UNDERSTANDING WINDOWS AZURE WEB SITES

There have been a lot of promises made about how cloud computing will change the software developer's life. To sort the chaff out, it's useful to step back and assess what you have grown accustomed to as you build, deploy, and manage websites. In that vein, let's remove cloud and Azure from the conversation for a moment, and define some of the main aspects of web development to which you have likely become accustomed to throughout your career. As a starting point, this discussion assumes that you have worked with "traditional" deployments to a server that you or your company owns and manages.

What are the advantages of running your own server? First of all, you have the freedom to pick whatever operating systems and languages you'll use and how you're going to implement them. Second, you can manage files at a low level, working right against the file system. Third, you have the capability to connect to databases from whichever vendor or open-source offering you choose — and speaking of open source, it's easy to kick-start a project using myriad templates, including CMS, blogging, shopping cart, payment processors, or other project templates available from the developer community. These are all valuable assets in your developer arsenal and they enable you to remain flexible as you address your clients' requirements.

However, I would be remiss to not identify the ramifications of running one's own server, and certainly we need to understand these implications as developers. First and foremost are the costs. If you're going to run your own server you must pay for the metal, the physical presence (whether on- or off-premises), and the bandwidth. There are also costs associated with power, cooling and Internet connectivity. You might even be inclined to purchase a great server, to allow for scaling.

But with good hardware alone are you really ready? Who's going to maintain the security patches? How will you handle load balancing? What if you want to incorporate a service bus layer, or improve performance overseas if your website takes off in Asia or Europe? You also have to consider redundancy, security, and caching; and even if you get all that right, when it's time to scale you will have to buy more hardware. I don't argue that having your own server in place isn't without its freedom, but it doesn't guarantee that you'll be home free!

Your website isn't going to write itself, so it would be great if the aforementioned list of potential limitations were available without the consequent list of costs and responsibilities. And this is exactly where Windows Azure Web Sites comes into play. It essentially removes the operating system and physical hardware of a traditional server from the equation while adding robustness and scalability. Well played, Windows Azure, well played.

Though you will have opportunity to scale later, the default configuration of a Windows Azure Web Site is the equivalent of a website you would create in IIS. There is a chunk of file system set aside for your app, and a portion of memory and processor utilization are sliced off for your application. A host header and corresponding DNS entry are aligned with the site so that you can start browsing right away. Your website is simply a set of files on a file system. Sounds familiar, doesn't it?

To the point of this topic, you need to know where the Web Sites product fits into the spectrum of Windows Azure offerings. If you have previous experience with cloud computing, you know there are many different approaches you can take; and with previous Windows Azure experience, you may choose to spin up a compute instance and walk through some deployment preparation and configuration.

Another approach would be to set up a VM with IIS running on it — but that parallels running on a server you own, and all the responsibilities noted earlier fall back on you!

Windows Azure Web Sites do indeed fall into the category of "compute," but they are now highlighted as a separate execution model. This model enables you to share IIS on a VM with other websites, each in its own app domain, and eventually scale up to a dedicated virtual machine or a bank of 10 virtual servers, each of which has 4 cores and 7GB of memory. You definitely have options.

UNDERSTANDING THE WINDOWS AZURE PORTAL

You're already aware that Windows Azure provides much more than just a way to deploy and manage websites, so it will come as no surprise to find a lot more tooling on the Windows Azure Portal than what you require to manage your application, but once you are comfortable with the layout you'll find that most options you need are fairly close at hand.

The main area of the window presents a list of all items on your account from all the feature areas, as shown in Figure 1-1. A command bar is located along the bottom, which updates itself to present options relevant to the area or item you've selected.

FIGURE 1-1

NOTE *The Management Portal has seen some great improvements over the last year and many changes have been ushered in. Your options in the portal may not exactly match those illustrated in Figure 1-1. As new features are released, you may be required to opt in to them through your account settings before the related menu items are made available in your portal.*

Selecting a feature from the left navigation pane, such as Web Sites, presents the list of items filtered to that feature, as shown in Figure 1-2, which helps you quickly find whatever items you may be looking for in a particular category. Note that the left navigation pane collapses into its icon representation to give you more real estate in the window as you select a particular item.

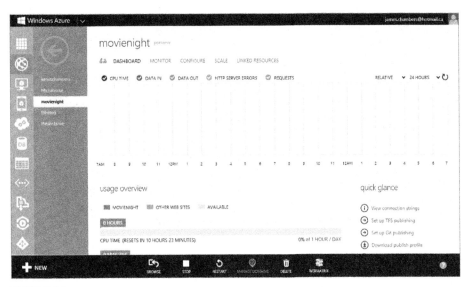

FIGURE 1-2

In addition to creating more real estate, selecting an item from the list by clicking on its name will take you to the dashboard for managing that item. Alternatively, you can select a row by clicking elsewhere on the row to highlight it, then use the context menu at the bottom of the screen to perform some of the basic state management commands that you may be familiar with from IIS. These operations and other related commands are described in detail later in this chapter, but first you'll need to create a site in order to display them in your portal.

CREATING A SIMPLE SITE

With Web Sites selected (the globe in the left-hand navigation menu), you can create a basic site by following these steps:

1. Click the New button in the context menu at the bottom of the screen. A fly-out menu will appear with three options for creating an Azure Web Site: Quick Create, Custom Create, or From Gallery, as shown in Figure 1-3.

2. Click Quick Create, which exposes a panel to name your site, as I've done. Pick a unique name by filling in the URL field and click the Create Web Site button to create your site.

    In Figure 1-3, you'll see a Region field that can also be provided. Microsoft provides a number of different regions in which your Azure Web Site can be created. As a general rule, select the region that is geographically closest to the people who you expect to use your website. However, the complete answer is not that simple. There are a couple of potential ramifications of your choice. The first is that you can have a maximum of 10 free Web Sites in any region. If you have 10 active free Web Sites in a single region, you will have to create your eleventh (and subsequent) Web Site in a different region.

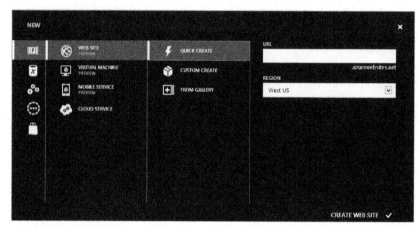

FIGURE 1-3

The second potential consideration relates to the scalability of a Web Site. As will be covered in Chapter 7, "Scaling, Configuring, and Monitoring Your Site," there are three levels of scalability supported by WAWS: Free, Shared, and Reserved. When you upgrade a Web Site to Reserved, then all of the Web Sites in the same region are also upgraded. As a result, when you determine the region in which your Web Site is being created, keep in mind whether you expected it to always be "free" or to grow into "reserved" at some point in the future.

You'll need to wait a few moments while Windows Azure spins up your website. Each new site creation process entails several stages, none of which require administrator interaction — namely, creating, deploying, and running.

After completion of the latter stage, you'll see your website in the portal.

3.   Click on the URL to launch it in a separate window. If you see the message shown in Figure 1-4 when you click the link, congratulations!

FIGURE 1-4

This default site won't win you any awards for web design and functionality, but it will serve as a proxy while you learn the essentials of managing a site. In Chapter 8, "Deploying and Configuring a Cloud Application," you'll look at an Azure Web Site with a little more oomph. This fledgling application will help you explore many of the real-world scenarios that most developers encounter as they grow their site.

MANAGING YOUR SITE FROM THE PORTAL

This section examines the management options in a little more detail. To follow along, you'll need to navigate to the dashboard of your site by walking through the following steps:

1. Close any browser windows that were opened when you were exploring the site you created in the previous section. Leave open the window containing the Windows Azure Management Portal.

2. Click the globe icon or Web Sites item in the left navigation pane. This will take you to the filtered list of websites that you have created.

3. Click the name of the website you just created to be taken to the dashboard for your site, which contains some options for getting started, as shown in Figure 1-5.

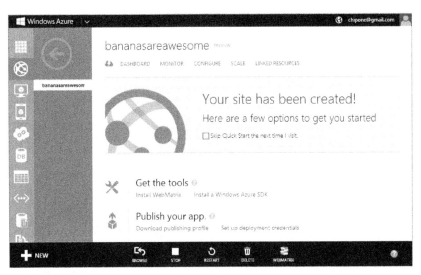

FIGURE 1-5

NOTE *When you start working with Windows Azure you may only have a few items in your list, and the All Items pivot may serve you well. This list will grow rapidly, however, especially as you use multiple features in concert, and the filtering provided by clicking on a menu item will help you easily navigate your Windows Azure assets.*

As mentioned earlier, the menu will collapse, giving you a little more working space in the portal. You can also easily switch between any websites you have created on your account, as the menu title area is converted to a list of the Web Sites that are part of your subscription.

Working with Notifications

As you carry out operations on the site, the portal does a pretty good job of keeping you up to date. Any list of the items in your account contains a status column for each row, which is updated in real time.

Figure 1-6 is an illustration of the working indicator in action. The icon lights up in the bottom-right corner of the portal, adjacent to the help icon (the question mark, seen in the bottom right corner of Figure 1-5). This icon lets you know that Windows Azure is working on completing an operation you started, even if you navigate to a different page in the portal.

FIGURE 1-6

Clicking the working indicator icon causes a progress panel similar to the one shown in Figure 1-7 to appear. The panel will contain relevant bits on the progress of the operations in your queue, and even more information can be exposed by clicking on the "detail" link in the panel. As commands transit through state to completion or error, you can track them here.

FIGURE 1-7

Modifying Application State

At this point, the menu at the bottom of the screen (see Figure 1-8) reflects the context of the selected site, displaying the state management options available for your application. This menu is referred to as the command bar or the "drawer." The commands you see here are always in the context of your current work area.

FIGURE 1-8

Keep in mind that having this context to the available operations will mean that sometimes an operation may not appear in the drawer. For example, the Start and Stop commands are only present when the site is either stopped or started, respectively.

➤ **Stop** — Prevents new requests from accessing the application and spins down the site. All outstanding requests are terminated. Take note, as this is different than the default behavior for Internet Information Services (IIS).

➤ **Start** — Prepares the web site for the first incoming request, but does not authoritatively start the site. Application initialization occurs when the first request reaches the website.

➤ **Restart** — Performs a stop operation followed by a start operation. Outstanding requests are terminated, the app domain is unloaded, leaving your application in a ready-to-start state. This is effectively the same as performing separate stop and start operations.

Performing Other Application Operations

Continuing with the command bar at the bottom of the screen, take a look at these other operations (see Figure 1-9) as they pertain to the context of your site, depending on your site configuration.

FIGURE 1-9

➤ **Browse** — Opens the website in a new browser window (or tab). If your application is "cold," it may take a moment to start. This operation has the technical side effect of changing your application's state when in the "ready" but not "started" state, as it counts as a first request to your site.

NOTE *WAWS has two types of "cold" states. The first is the type that many ASP.NET developers are used to in IIS. After a period of inactivity (typically 20 minutes), IIS will shut down the process that handles the requests for a particular website. The first subsequent request will cause the process to restart, but will typically take a little longer than average to process.*

The second type of "cold" state occurs when a Web Site is deactivated due to inactivity. This is done to help preserve the quotas that Windows Azure imposes on Free and Shared mode Web Sites. As with the IIS "cold" state, there will be a delay when the first request is received. However, because the Web Site needs to be reactivated, it will actually take even longer than the IIS warm-up time.

➤ **Manage Domains** — Reveals a popup window that enables you to configure which domains are associated with the current website. Note that you have to perform some additional steps in order for this feature to be enabled, which are covered in Chapter 7, "Scaling, Configuring, and Monitoring Your Site." When your site is properly configured, this command item will appear, as was shown in Figure 1-2.

➤ **Web Matrix** — Opens the Azure Web Site locally for editing in the WebMatrix Integrated Development Environment (IDE). If you don't have the IDE installed, it will be bootstrapped as part of this operation. The website files are downloaded from Windows Azure to your local file system and you can edit the site locally before pushing any changes.

Deleting a Site

As a careful reader who has been closely inspecting all the wonderful artwork in the book and reading attentively, you likely noticed that I did not mention the Delete button in the previous set of commands. That's because there is a little more going on with delete — it's worth noting separately, as this is one of the marked differences from hosting a website on your own server.

Remember that your Azure Web Site is very much like what you would have on IIS; there's an entry on a virtual machine somewhere that serves requests to your clients, and a set of files that are referenced as part of the configuration. Unlike your traditional IIS deployment, however, your web site has a number of other details attached to it that are also deleted when you delete the site. These details extend beyond the standard configuration of a website in IIS and include the DNS entries, related host headers and logs, as well as post-deployment configuration that you may have set up, such as connection strings, application settings, or the scaling options of your site. Among the most important of these attached details are the files that make up your application and enable your site to tick. When you delete a site on Windows Azure Web Sites, all your application files are gone for good.

WARNING *This brings up a very important related point: Do not count on Windows Azure Web Site (or any deployed website) as a form of source control! Although you could handle this manually, keeping track of which version of your site exists where, imagine the horror of losing hours of work or damaging a relationship with a customer because you accidentally pulled or pushed the wrong version of your site when working with a publishing tool! You'll look at several alternatives for managing your files that outline some best practices to help prevent this in Chapter 3, "Managing Deployments via Source Control."*

Setting Your Deployment Credentials

Although you have already logged into the portal and tied your Microsoft Account to your Azure subscription, certain deployment procedures in this book require a different set of credentials. This is because some protocols (such as FTP) and third-party providers (such as Git) do not support Microsoft Accounts.

You can configure your subscription-wide username and password through the "Reset deployment credentials" link from the dashboard of any Windows Azure Web Site. As shown in Figure 1-10 the link appears under the quick glance section of the page.

FIGURE 1-10

Selecting this link allows you to originally set and subsequently reset your credentials as required, as you can see in Figure 1-11.

New user name and password

Git and FTP cannot use your Windows account to authenticate, so this dialog lets you specify a user name and password that can be used when using those technologies.

This user name and password can be used to deploy to any web site in your subscription. You do not need to set credentials for every web site that you create.

USER NAME

Your-Name-Here

NEW PASSWORD

••••••••••••••••

CONFIRM PASSWORD

••••••••••••••••

FIGURE 1-11

SUMMARY

At first blush Windows Azure Web Sites may just look like another hosting option for your website — with options and management features that will be familiar to most developers working on the .NET stack. While it has its familiarities, it also has the benefit of not being tied to a specific piece of hardware, and the ability to leverage other aspects of cloud computing down the road, particularly scalability and high availability.

This chapter's coverage of the Azure Portal should enable you to create and locate sites, and access the site management commands, with confidence.

Managing the state of your site is probably a familiar concept, and you have seen how Azure compares to a more traditional hosting environment. Although the differences in how you create and delete sites are relatively minor, you do need to be aware of them, and which pieces of your configuration will be affected as you perform certain operations.

2 Moving an Application to the Cloud

IN THIS CHAPTER:

- ➤ An overview of publishing options when moving a website to Windows Azure
- ➤ Setting and reviewing credentials and server hostnames
- ➤ Selecting the best deployment strategy

WROX.COM CODE DOWNLOADS FOR THIS CHAPTER

Please note that all the code examples in this chapter are available as a part of this chapter's code download on the book's website at www.wrox.com on the Download Code tab. You'll be publishing all the related code from two of the projects in the download:

Basic Site Publish Files — This is a pre-baked deployment ready to push to the cloud, based off of the SimpleSite solution output.

SimpleSite — This is a Visual Studio 2012 solution that you will use as a publishing exercise.

Many friends of mine enjoy freely cracking open their computers and upgrading parts between coding sessions, but I would argue that there is a difference between being a software developer and a computer hardware technician. Sure, the roles are often blurred — anyone in my programming circles is more apt to diagnose a driver issue than most other professionals I know — but building and deploying new servers is outside our area of expertise.

I've spent my fair share of time in the server room; but as someone who truly loves the art of software development, I'd have to afford the reader that, for me, "compiler" is a preferred tool over "Phillips 2." And when my intentions are to use an evening of my free time to pick up some new library or utility, or otherwise sharpen my coding skills, I don't want to carry the burden of server maintenance at the same time.

Therefore, while I do tend to remain as far as possible from the rack and chassis these days, I have found great pleasure in adopting Windows Azure as my new favorite web server administrator. It takes only a moment to cut a new project with all the bits you need to deploy, monitor, and scale your site already in place. Windows Azure provides a fully upgraded environment with service packs applied — in moments — with just a few button clicks. Recent improvements in deployment scheduling also mean that Azure supports the latest .NET builds within days or weeks of general availability.

All of this is to say that you get quite a few personal benefits when using Azure in your deployment pipeline — not to mention potential corporate benefits — and you're here now, looking to push your app up to the sky, so let's get started! The deployment examples in this chapter make use of a trivial application that simply shows contact information for 25 random, fictitious people. These exercises don't require any advanced configuration or any database connectivity.

In Chapter 8, "Deploying and Configuring Cloud Application," you'll have a look at a more complete example that allows you to explore the features covered in this and the other chapters.

UPLOADING YOUR WEB SITE VIA FTP

Long before users were bestowed OS-integrated FTP support, web application developers were making use of the command-line version of FTP to synchronize the server with our latest output. In fact, FTP likely predates most of today's web developers themselves! With roots dating back over four decades, the protocol has been used in many different and varied scenarios and still provides much usefulness in today's modern networks.

Gathering the Basics

There are only three prerequisites for publishing via FTP: knowing the name of the FTP deployment server to which you're connecting, the subdomain name for the Web Site, and your username and password.

Provided you've configured your publishing credentials, setting up to leverage FTP is fairly straightforward. For the purpose of this example, you'll work from the pre-baked version of a website that is ready to deploy, after an initial push with a single "hello world" sample.

There are a couple of details you should note at this point. The URL for the FTP Deployment server is located under the quick glance sidebar in the Dashboard of your website as shown in Figure 2-1. Your hostname will take on a format similar to the following:

```
ftp://waws-prod-blu-001.ftp.azurewebsites.windows.net
```

FIGURE 2-1

Also located in the quick glance side bar is the name of your deployment/FTP user. You may find that all server endpoints across your subscription are identical, but the user you log in with sorts out the home directory for each particular FTP session. Your username is in the format sitename\user, where user is the name you specified when you created your publishing credentials. If you don't recall what they are, you can reset them by following the steps in the section titled "Setting Your Deployment Credentials" in Chapter 1.

Connecting to the Server

Those of you who have previously worked with FTP may have a more elegant software package than working from Windows Explorer to connect and manage your files. You can perform the steps here in your preferred FTP client if you choose, or you can use the operating system's built-in support for FTP. The latter approach, which is generally the more cumbersome choice, is what you'll use for the purpose of this exercise, but feel free to follow along in whichever software you ultimately decide to use.

To make it easy to get started, follow these steps:

1. Copy your FTP hostname from your site's dashboard to the clipboard.

2. Open a copy of Windows Explorer (press the Start key+E) and paste the hostname into the address bar. When you press Enter, Windows will try to connect to the server, at which point you'll see the dialog shown in Figure 2-2.

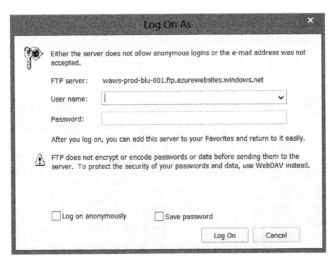

FIGURE 2-2

3. Fill in your credentials and click the Log On option to complete the connection. After you are logged in, you will see the two folders that are created for you each time you provision a Web Site — namely, LogFiles and site.

4. Navigate into the site folder, and finally into the wwwroot folder, where you'll find a single file called `hostingstart.html`. This is the directory you'll target when you deploy the application.

NOTE *A heads up on security: Although FTP is provided as a convenience, it may not meet the security requirements of your organization. Remember that FTP sends your credentials via clear text — that's right, no encryption — so anyone who might be "listening" to the traffic on your connection could exploit your username and password. For this reason, Azure provides a secure FTP (sFTP) endpoint for users who elect to use this as part of their workflow.*

Keep this FTP directory open because you're going to come back to it in just a moment.

Validating a Connection

Your sample Windows Azure Web Site is already live at this point and a default document is prepped and waiting for visitors to view. You can see this by opening your browser and navigating to the website, which uses the following naming convention:

`http://your-app-name.azurewebsites.net`

Therefore, for an application named "MovieNight," the address is simply as follows:

`http://movienight.azurewebsites.net`

You should see a page similar to Figure 2-3 confirming that your application is running on WAWS.

FIGURE 2-3

You can change what users see when they arrive at your site by adding a new page to this directory. This section doesn't get too fancy here — it just sticks with the bare bones to demonstrate the process:

1. Open Notepad and add the following code to a new document:

```
</html>
  <body>
    <p>Hello, cloud!</p>
  </body>
</html>
```

2. Save the file to your desktop and name it "index.html." If you prefer, you can save this to another easily accessible location on your computer.

3. Locate the FTP directory that you left open in the previous section. If you no longer have it open, reopen it now and log back in.

4. Copy and paste the file into the FTP directory. This will leave you with two files in the directory: hostingstart.html, which was created for you, and the new index.html that you've just added.

5. Open your web browser and navigate back to your site. Use the previously discussed convention of http://your-app-name.azurewebsites.net.

Congratulations, you should now see your lovely handiwork!

NOTE *The file named* index.html *takes precedence over one named* hostingstart .html *in the same directory because of the default configuration in Windows Azure Web Sites. For more information on how to control the default document, please see Chapter 7, "Scaling, Configuring and Monitoring Your Site."*

Publishing the "Real" Site

Okay, so all you've really done here is push a text file, proving that the basic HTML skills are still in check. Now you want to see a true site — something beyond brochureware — live and kicking from that remote box. Nonetheless, you have picked up the basics of publishing via FTP through Windows Explorer:

➤ Connecting to the FTP server

➤ Locating your website directory

➤ Copying the files to the server

These are the same basic principles you will apply for subsequent pushes of your application. Let's now put those principles in action and get some real content up there.

The code sample download contains a directory titled Basic Site Publishing Files, and within it another directory called wwwroot. You want to copy and paste all those files into the FTP directory, which results in a folder resembling the output denoted in Figure 2-4.

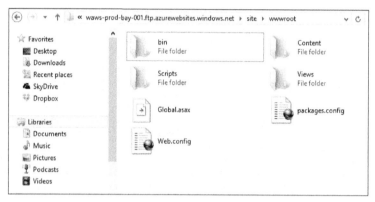

FIGURE 2-4

Browse back to your site address and have a look around. Welcome to the cloud!

PUBLISHING FROM WEBMATRIX

Microsoft WebMatrix provides a seamless development and deployment experience with built-in support for your Microsoft Account credentials. This means that it is aware of your Azure account and the Web Sites that you have provisioned, and has the ability to create and stage new websites for you. It's not a traditional tool in a .NET developer's toolkit, but it does have deep integration, support for open-source projects, an active community of developers who are building extensions, and an overall pleasant experience to experiment with.

To follow along with this section you must download the sample code for the book, which contains the files required to publish via WebMatrix.

Deploying Your Site for the First Time

Here's how simple it is to take the same site you used in the previous FTP example and publish it using WebMatrix:

1. Open WebMatrix and log in using your Windows Azure credentials. The login link is in the top-right corner. If you have previously logged in, WebMatrix will remember your credentials.

2. Choose Open ⇨ Folder from the welcome screen and select the folder containing the basic site publishing files. This is the wwwroot folder located in Basic Site Publishing Files, which is in your code download.

3. Click the Publish command in the Home ribbon. This will open the Publish Your Site dialog.

4. Select Create a New Site and fill in the required information. Azure needs you to name the site, choose a region, and associate the site with a new or existing database. You can create a new database if you like, but you won't be using this resource for the purpose of this exercise. Figure 2-5 illustrates a completed example. Click OK to continue, and WebMatrix will download the related publishing profile for your site.

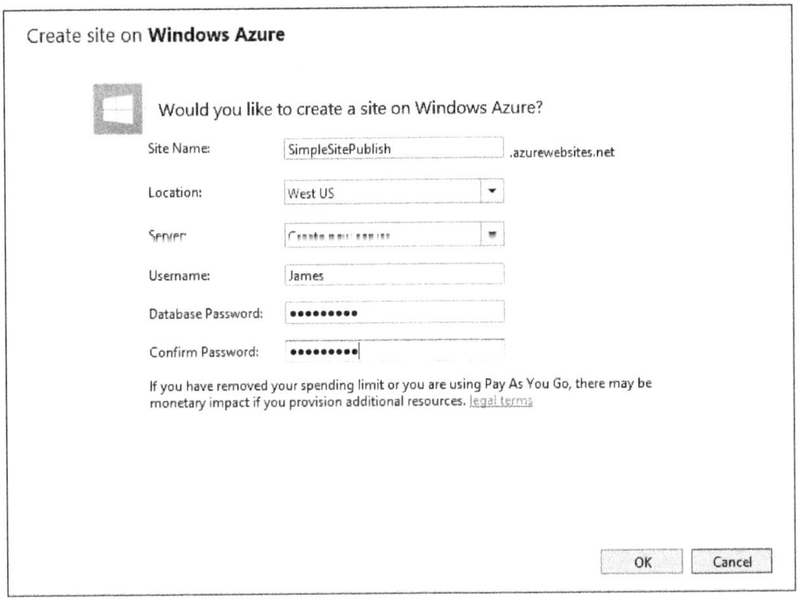

Create site on **Windows Azure**

Would you like to create a site on Windows Azure?

Site Name: SimpleSitePublish .azurewebsites.net

Location: West US

Server: Create new server

Username: James

Database Password: ●●●●●●●●

Confirm Password: ●●●●●●●●

If you have removed your spending limit or you are using Pay As You Go, there may be monetary impact if you provision additional resources. legal terms

OK   Cancel

FIGURE 2-5

NOTE *The name of your Web Site is used to create a subdomain of azurewebsites.net. You might have noticed this in your site's URL. For this reason, all Windows Azure Web Sites require a name that is unique among all the other sites hosted on Azure, and you will get an error message if enter a name that has already been selected. But don't worry if your coveted name is no longer available as a subdomain; we'll explore adding a custom domain name to your site in Chapter 7, "Scaling, Configuring, and Monitoring Your Site."*

5. Complete the test deployment by clicking Continue, and Continue again once the tests are complete. WebMatrix will ensure that the basic components of the site are compatible with the Azure Web Site and display the results. You are not required to do this step and can skip it if you like, but I recommend trying it out at least once to familiarize yourself with the process. This simple step can help catch deployment problems before they occur!

6. Review the Publish Preview screen. This contains the type of information that WebMatrix presents to you as you begin the publish process on each iteration. In future sessions you will usually see far fewer files; the initial deployment has to upload all the assets of the project, while subsequent deployments perform a differential upload, so only those files that have changed will be shown in the screen (and sent to the Web Site).

7. Click Continue to complete your deployment. The dialog will close and you'll see a yellow alert panel at the bottom of the screen. This panel reports on progress as WebMatrix processes changes on your site.

When all files are in sync — the first deployment can take a few minutes — you'll see the confirmation depicted in Figure 2-6 and you can click the link to view your site.

FIGURE 2-6

Publishing Changes to the Site

Now that the site is associated with a Windows Azure Web Site instance, changes that you make can easily be identified, and synchronizing the site goes more quickly. Try it out by following these steps:

1. In the project structure, navigate to the Home directory under Views and open the Index.cshtml file.

2. Change the H2 title tag of the page to something of your liking. The tag is located near the top of the file and looks like this:

    ```
    <h2>Index</h2>
    ```

3. Click Publish on the Home ribbon.

4. Review the changes that will be published. Note that this time around, only one file has changed and needs to be uploaded to the site.

5. Click Continue to complete the deployment. The alert panel is displayed again and shows the progress of deployment.

That's the basics! You can now refresh your site and see any changes you've made.

PUBLISHING THROUGH DROPBOX

Dropbox is a cloud-based file storage system that makes it easy to move files around from computers, tablets, phones, and through the web interface. It started with a private beta and grew to millions of users, and its creators recently announced that Dropbox users were uploading more than one billion files per day. So, yeah...they're popular. Chances are good you already have a Dropbox account; if not, it's easy to set one up. This section describes an easy way to move project files to a cloud application server.

Before you get started, please ensure that you have a Dropbox account set up and that you have downloaded the appropriate software for your operating system. Dropbox users will already be familiar with the client software that you use to keep your files in sync with your cloud storage account.

To follow along with this section you must download the sample code for the book, which contains the files required to publish via Dropbox.

Associating Your Web Site with a Dropbox Folder

Because Dropbox is not a Microsoft product and doesn't exist as part of the Windows Azure offering, you first need to set up a trust between the services. Start by creating a new site from your Azure portal as you did in "Creating a Simple Site" in Chapter 1, and then follow these steps:

1. Navigate to the dashboard of your site in the Azure portal. For the purposes of these steps, let's presume that the name of your site is "movienight." Just remember that you need to pick a unique name and use that throughout this exercise.

2. Under the Quick Glance section of the dashboard, select "Set up deployment from source control." This reveals a prompt asking "Where is your source code?"

3. Select Dropbox from the list of source control providers and click the Next arrow.

4. Sign in (if required), review the prompt from Dropbox, and click Allow. Dropbox provides an authentication and association window to confirm that you indeed wish to set up a link between Azure and your Dropbox account, to which you'll need to be signed in.

5. Choose a new folder in the "Set up publishing" dialog and name the new folder. By default, Azure gives the folder the same name as your site name. In this example, that means that the folder would be named "movienight." This makes it easy to identify the site to which you're publishing.

When you are done you'll see a confirmation similar to that in Figure 2-7, letting you know that everything completed successfully. You're now published and online. Congrats!

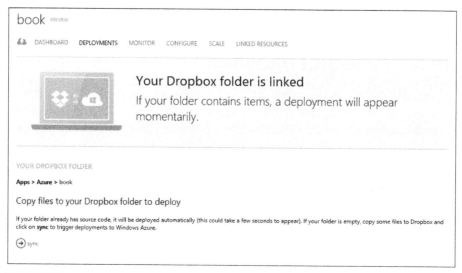

FIGURE 2-7

Pushing Files to the Cloud through Dropbox

Dropbox integrates directly with your operating system so well that it's hard to tell that it isn't just another file location on your computer. In the preceding steps, Dropbox created a directory called Apps in the root of your Dropbox folder, and a folder for Azure nested within it. Inside Azure is yet another folder that bears the name of the folder you created earlier — by default, the name of your web site, which for this example would be "movienight." Time to deploy your site:

1. Open Windows Explorer and locate the folder for your website by selecting Dropbox ➪ Apps ➪ Azure.

2. Open another Windows Explorer and locate the wwwroot folder inside of Simple Site Publishing Files from the code download for the book.

3. Copy all files from the wwwroot folder to your website folder in Dropbox. At this point I recommend getting yourself a drink! Otherwise, you can log into Dropbox and wait for all the files to show up. It takes a while to sync.

4. Navigate to your website's dashboard in your Azure portal.

5. Click the Deployments tab, and then click the Sync button. It will take a moment to capture all the files, and the view of the deployments screen will change to show you your active deployment.

6. Return to your dashboard, and click on your site URL under the Quick Glance section.

If you make changes to your site in the Dropbox folder on your machine, all you have to do is hit that Sync button again and your site will be updated. Feel free to give it a try!

As you can see, this model whereby Windows Azure "pulls" your site from another location can be pretty powerful, and the sharp reader will be wondering about the list of deployments that is amended with each sync operation you perform. Hang tight, you'll be working with deployments in depth in Chapter 3, "Managing Deployments via Source Control."

GOING TO THE CLOUD WITH VISUAL STUDIO 2012

The last piece is one that I put in the game changer category. Publishing to Windows Azure through Visual Studio 2012 has all but eliminated any barriers for any experienced developer who wants to try running a website on the cloud. This could be the single most enticing feature that will draw you in and make you want to experiment with Windows Azure Web Sites, if you haven't already done so.

Now that I've set the bar so unrealistically high that you are likely having a hard time believing it, I'm going to walk you through the steps and hopefully gain some face in the process!

To follow along with this section you must download the sample code for the book, which contains the files required to publish with Visual Studio 2012.

Downloading Your Publishing Profile

The key to this magic show is the publishing profile that is exposed on the dashboard of any Windows Azure Web Site. This is an XML file that gives Visual Studio the instructions it needs to complete a deployment to Azure. You can create your own XML file and add it to your project manually, but Windows Azure Web Sites and Visual Studio 2012 give you an easy alternative: Download the pre-configured settings and easily import them into your project.

Pop back into your portal and use Quick Create to add another site to your account, and then follow along with these steps:

1. Go to the dashboard for your site in the Azure portal.

2. Click the "Download publish profile" link under the Quick Glance section of the dashboard. When the browser prompts you to save the file, select a location you'll be able to remember in the next step.

Registering the Publishing Profile with Your Project

You don't have to create the project from scratch, but you can if you like. For a head start, there is a solution entitled "SimpleSite" in the code download for the book. This is the source code for the files you've been deploying so far throughout this chapter. The following steps take you through the publishing process for the SimpleSite solution, but it's an easy transition to use your own site in its place.

1. Locate and open the `SimpleSite.sln` solution file in Visual Studio 2012.

2. Select Build ⇨ Publish from the menu. Visual Studio will launch the Publish Web dialog.

3. Switch to the Profile tab if you're not already there, and click the button labeled Import next to the profile selection dropdown.

4. Navigate to and select the publishing profile you downloaded in the previous section. You'll see all the credentials and connection information you need automatically filled in for you. You can click the Validate Connection button to assert that you have a valid configuration.

5. Click the Publish button. Visual Studio takes care of the heavy lifting for you.

From this point forward, all you have to do is click Build ⇨ Publish to push updates to your site. And the real value of using this deployment mechanism? You can add multiple publishing profiles to your project and deploy on a whim to any of them.

The publishing profile is the same format that is used by Web Deploy and it can be incorporated into your physical servers as well, meaning you can deploy as easily to your test environment as you can to a scalable, cloud-based production server running on Windows Azure. You can even leverage these profiles as part of your continuous deployment process or otherwise in your build scripts.

SELECTING A DEPLOYMENT STRATEGY

It's fairly trivial to work with tools like FTP and DropBox to deploy your site, both of which provide a method that is as straightforward as using the file system to copy files. WebMatrix and the Visual Studio IDE give you a method of publishing from directly within the tools you're using to create your site. There can be great benefit from being able to directly push files to the cloud, but how do you keep track of changes? What happens when you work with other team members? Will you be expected to support multiple versions of your site?

These techniques let you play with the metal, so to speak, and grind files out quickly and effectively with the caveat that you're unable to really take your deployments to the next level. It's hard to work with other folks on your team without overwriting files and losing work, or worse, even rendering your site inoperable. There is no way to roll back to a previous version — or even track previous versions — and all of a sudden you start to realize that "quick" and "effective" might not be what you're looking for.

Truthfully, publishing as illustrated in this chapter is quickly outgrown by the serious hobbyist and professionals alike. You're going to need to take control of your source and start using repositories. If you're working with other team members, on open source projects or even alone, using a source control repository really opens the door to some deployment methods that pair up really nicely with Windows Azure Web Sites. If you're looking to build a strategy for deployment it should not include copying and pasting files, nor should it include any process which permanently overwrites previous work.

Unfortunately, all of the techniques demonstrated thus far allow you to fall into those traps. Fortunately, you're about to learn how to tie your code base hosted in any one of several source control providers to the automated deployment facilities of Windows Azure. Chapter 3 will cover this ground and give you some solid footing as you move past these basic concepts and towards an environment that fits most development realities.

SUMMARY

There are almost as many ways to get your web application up on the cloud as there are ways to say "hello," and you're only halfway through them! You should now feel pretty comfortable using several different tools to deploy your site and keep it up to date.

Be it simple operations as basic as copying files for FTP or Dropbox, using more complete tooling and authoring environments such as WebMatrix, or building a solution in a fully featured IDE like Visual Studio, you've seen how the friction related to deployment has been significantly lessened. So it's time to start experimenting!

Ultimately, chances are good that you'll be working with more mature sites, sites built through the effort of a team, with a distributed group, or for clients that work offsite; and for those types of projects, you'll likely need to leverage some kind of source control, the subject of the next chapter.

3 Managing Deployments via Source Control

IN THIS CHAPTER:

- ➤ Associating a version control system with your Azure account
- ➤ Using source control repositories to publish Azure Web Sites
- ➤ Working with different versions of a previously deployed code base

WROX.COM CODE DOWNLOADS FOR THIS CHAPTER

Please note that all the code examples in this chapter are available as a part of this chapter's code download on the book's website at www.wrox.com on the Download Code tab. You'll be publishing all the related code from the following project in the download:

SimpleSite — This is a Visual Studio 2012 solution that you will use as a publishing exercise throughout this chapter.

It is often said that the only good code is shipped code. Until code is shipped, users gain no benefit from our efforts. And on too many occasions, the time between development and deployment into production can be measured in weeks and months. So how great would it be to have code shipped as soon as it's checked in? This is an idea that has been gaining support for quite a while. Support not just in terms of people approving of the idea, but also in the number and quality of tools used to actually deliver on it. Developers can add Windows Azure Web Sites to the list of tools that help achieve this laudable goal.

Developers don't go out of their way to make their deployment process intentionally more complex. They don't add extra tools to their toolkit for the heck of it. They have no desire to make it difficult for the team to work together. The process of developing code, integrating new functions into the application, and performing tests is already challenging to do. There is no benefit to making the points of interaction among the team members worse.

And yes, the build or deployment process is often a point of tension on many teams. Perhaps the build is fragile. One small piece out of place and tests start to fail. Or maybe the build is inconsistent, showing failure one moment and success immediately afterwards. Any situation like this is one that development teams want to avoid.

Typically, at the onset of a project, someone will lead the effort to put the build together. They wire up the compilation of the separate projects and create scripts for the deployment and testing steps. This can be intimidating. And to make it worse, the most typical pattern has the build changing on a regular basis over the development period as more and more functionality is added.

Many good patterns exist for creating a seamless build and deployment experience. If your build and deployment systems are not causing pain in your daily work, there may be very little business value in changing it. This chapter should not be viewed as a demand to rewrite your deployment process. If, however, the only continuity in your build process is "stress," then it might be time to consider an alternative approach.

As your development toolkit has grown and matured, so has the general landscape for the build process. Continuous Integration servers are equipped with web-based front ends that are capable of monitoring changes to source control, checking out code, executing build scripts, performing automatic acceptance tests, staging deployments to multiple servers, as well as myriad other tasks. These systems will not be perfect for every team, every scenario, or perhaps even for your project requirements, but they are good to be aware of so that when you are ready, you're equipped with the pieces you need to deliver a timely and comprehensive solution.

Now, the fact that Windows Azure can integrate easily and rather seamlessly into your continuous deployment process won't solve all your problems. But it does mean that Azure is a solid choice for a deployment target. And as an added benefit, configuring Azure and your build environment to accomplish this is not as intimidating as you might first think. After looking at the basics of working with source control systems, this chapter discusses the components of this process that make it easier to automate the juicy bits.

UNDERSTANDING PREREQUISITES

For most of the exercises that follow, you will be required to provide credentials in the Windows Azure portal for external source control systems. Each of these systems requires a varying degree of configuration and may require tool installation or shell extensions in order for you to work with them on your machine.

The focus of this chapter is to help you understand how source control tools (specifically the deployment components of those tools) allow for integration with Windows Azure Web Sites. That means that this chapter does not provide a comprehensive guide to installing, configuring, or managing your choice of source control. That is well beyond the scope of this chapter and this book. The assumption is that you have already selected a source control tool; this chapter covers four popular tool choices and how they work with WAWS.

You should have a good understanding of your tools of choice, the ability to check in code changes, and familiarity with creating branches and merging code as required. Using a variety of tools, I will demonstrate how diverse this process can be, but the examples will not serve as a tutorial for managing your source tree.

Finally, you should be comfortable with creating new Azure Web Sites and moving around the Windows Azure portal — specifically, with using the command bar and navigating to the dashboard of the website you're working with.

PUBLISHING FROM SOURCE CONTROL

In Chapter 2 you had a quick look at publishing from Dropbox. It is straightforward enough, and while it maintains history on files and integrates nicely into modern operating systems, it is missing some critical aspects of source control when used on its own. Although it is possible to create composite solutions — Git or Mercurial over Dropbox, for example — they rarely satisfy more than single-user requirements, and even then ideally only for backup and redundancy. Therefore, as simple as it is to set up Dropbox with Windows Azure Web Sites, it's probably not a real-world solution for your team. The following sections describe how to configure WAWS publishing from GitHub, CodePlex, Bitbucket, and Team Foundation Service.

Publishing from GitHub

GitHub is one of the fastest-growing hosts of open-source software projects, enabling private or public collaboration within organizations, between individuals and as a community. Though there is a for-fee model, you can make as many public repositories as you like, fork code from existing efforts, and contribute to projects created by others.

From Windows Azure Web Sites you are able to connect your site to any GitHub project associated with your account. This includes any public or private repositories you've created, as well as projects that you've forked from other sources. Better still, you can select the branch to be associated with your website, which allows for great flexibility in running multiple environments and deployment versions. Using a custom deployment engine, Windows Azure Web Sites will download code after a check-in, build your solution, and deploy your updated site automatically.

To get started, you'll need to set up a local repository and put some code in it. This section provides instructions assuming you'll be using GitHub for Windows as your client software. GitHub for Windows is an excellent GitHub client with a very streamlined UI that should feel right at home in your Windows environment. If you prefer to use another client, you should be able to tailor the process accordingly:

1. From the home screen in GitHub for Windows, create a new repository using the add button located at the top center of the screen. When you are done, open the repository in GitHub for Windows.

2. From File Explorer, copy the files for the Simple Site into your repository's local directory. The site solution is located in the Basic Site Publishing Files folder of the code download.

3. Return to the GitHub client to commit and publish your changes. You'll need to write a short note to describe your commit as required by the software — "Initial Commit" is fine — and then click Commit, followed by the sync button at the top of the client.

At this point your source code has a home on GitHub. All you need to do now is teach Windows Azure Web Sites how to deal with your repository:

1. Create a new website using the Quick Create template. You can create a new website from anywhere in the portal by clicking the New link in the command bar.

2. From the website dashboard, click the link to "Set up deployment from source control." This is located under the Quick Glance area of the dashboard.

3. Select GitHub from the list of providers and click the next arrow.

4. Authorize the application. GitHub prompts you to let you know that Azure will have permission to read your public and private repositories. Review the details and grant Azure access by clicking the Authorize app button.

5. Select the repository from the list and specify your branch. The dropdown will contain a list of Git repositories that are available to you, grouped by organization. The master branch is set as the default for you.

6. Click the checkmark to complete the association. You'll see a message similar to the one shown in Figure 3-1, letting you know that the link is being established.

FIGURE 3-1

You'll need to let Azure plug away as it creates the link (which is actually a type of service hook called a WebHook), clones the repository, compiles your solution, and deploys your site. The process is soon completed, with the current version of your source code showing as the active deployment. You can click the Browse button in the command bar to see the site.

NOTE *The WebHook won't always clone your repository, though it will be required the first time you associate your site with source control. After the initial clone, Azure just pulls against the repository to update the relevant files for any subsequent deployment.*

Publishing from CodePlex

CodePlex is a hosting site provided free of charge from Microsoft for open-source projects. It allows easy collaboration and multiple options for source control, so publishing from CodePlex is a bit of a meta-operation, as you can choose your client and source control platform from an array of options.

In order to enable support for your website to build and deploy from CodePlex, you'll need to have your project in the following state:

➤   Your project must use Git or Mercurial as the source control provider.

➤   Your project must have source checked in.

➤   You must have already published your project.

You can use the following steps to start from a newly created CodePlex project or adapt them as required to fit your project's status:

NOTE *Git Bash, referred to in the upcoming steps, is a command-line tool that can be used to manipulate Git repositories and source code. It is installed at the same time as Git. Git Bash is not the only mechanism available to clone a repository from CodePlex. Others, such as Source Tree, are freely available for download from the Internet. It is, however, included with Git and so it doesn't require any additional setup on your computer. That is its reason for being used in these steps.*

---

1.   Create a new project on CodePlex. You'll need to be signed in, and your project needs to be uniquely named.

2.   Navigate to the Source Code tab on your project. There will be no changesets here, as the project is still fresh.

3.   Capture the clone URL for your project to the clipboard. You can reveal the URL by clicking the Clone submenu.

4.   Using Git Bash, clone the repository from CodePlex. Use the following commands, substituting your proper project name and local working directory. Leave Git Bash open when you are done.

    ```
    git clone https://git01.codeplex.com/YourProjectName YourLocalDirectory
    cd YourLocalDirectory
    ```

5.   Use File Explorer to copy the Simple Site into the Git repository you just created. The site solution is located in the Basic Site Publishing Files folder of the code download.

6.   Commit your changes and push to CodePlex from Git Bash. You can use the following commands to add the files to the repository, create your initial commit, and complete the push:

```
git add .
git commit -m 'initial commit'
git push -u origin master
```

NOTE *If you have not previously saved your credentials for CodePlex, Git will prompt you for your username and password for operations such as clone and push. You will need to use the same username and password that you use to log into the CodePlex website.*

You'll see all the files scroll by as the operation completes, and you will be able to browse the code in CodePlex immediately.

As shown in Figure 3-2, publishing your project also requires a number of other elements. In addition to pushing your first set of code, you'll need to edit your home page, select one of the open-source licensing models available on the site, and finalize your project summary.

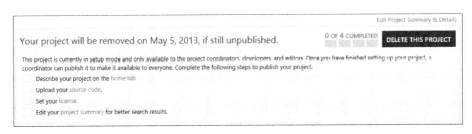

FIGURE 3-2

Complete each of those requirements, then follow these steps in your Azure portal to connect to CodePlex for automatic deployments:

1. Create a new website using the Quick Create template. You can create a new website from anywhere in the portal by clicking the New link in the command bar.

2. From the website dashboard, click the link to "Set up deployment from source control." This is located under the Quick Glance area of the dashboard.

3. Select CodePlex from the list and click the next arrow.

4. Authorize the application. Review the details of the permissions you're granting Azure and click the Authorize button.

5. Select the repository from the list. The dropdown will contain all published sites that are bound to Git or Mercurial source control.

6. Click the checkmark to complete the association.

It doesn't take long for things to happen from here. Azure will scoop up the latest check-in, build your solution, and then copy the output from the build to the active deployment for your site. Click the Browse link in the command bar to launch the site.

Publishing from Bitbucket

Originally tied to Mercurial, Bitbucket added support to the popular Git repository system in 2011, offering an array of integration features — with everything from other source control systems to social networks. The system enables you to maintain private and public repositories, fork and clone other people's projects, perform code reviews, track issues, and more.

Because of the support for Git, you can leverage the same source code directory that you used for publishing to CodePlex:

1. Create a new repository from your Bitbucket account and capture the Git endpoint to the clipboard. You can see the URL for your repository on the repository's Overview page.

2. From Git Bash, switch to the directory you created in the previous exercise. Use the following command, with the correct path:

    ```
    cd YourLocalDirectory
    ```

3. Add the remote repository for Bitbucket and push your commits. Use the following commands, replacing the URL with the one you copied to the clipboard in step 1:

    ```
    git remote add bitbucket https://username@bitbucket.org/username
    /YourSiteName.git
    git push -u bitbucket --all
    ```

Your final session from Git Bash will look something like Figure 3-3, with the obvious bits reflecting your path, username, and project name.

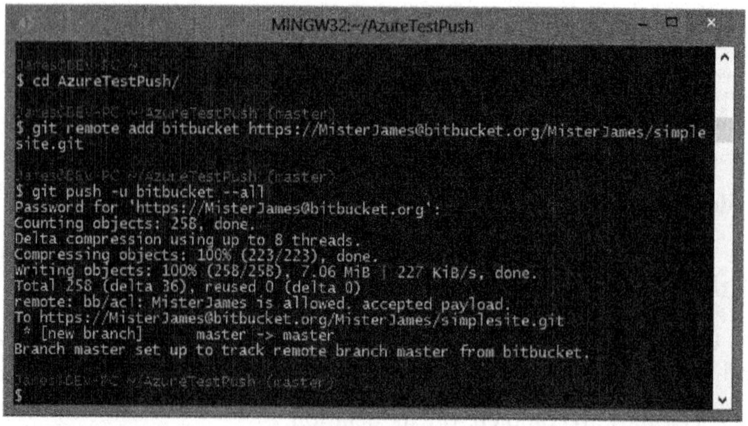

FIGURE 3-3

Now that your code has a comfy new place to hang out on Bitbucket, the final step is to get Windows Azure Web Sites chatting with the source repository. The steps are very similar to the other Git-based control systems:

1.   Log in to the Azure Portal and create a new website using the Quick Create template. You can create a new website from anywhere in the portal by clicking the New link in the command bar.

2.   From the website dashboard, click the link to "Set up deployment from source control." This is located under the Quick Glance area of the dashboard.

3.   Select Bitbucket from the list and click the next arrow. You will be prompted to enter your credentials to log into your Bitbucket account.

4.   Authorize the application. Review the details of the permissions you're granting Azure — read and write permissions on both private and public repositories — and click the "Grant access" button.

5.   Select the repository from the dropdown list and then select a branch. You can choose any repository that your account has permission to view, and any branch in that repository.

6.   Click the checkmark to complete the association.

NOTE *The Git-based repositories are configured with a POST URL when you create the association with your Windows Azure Web Site. The Git control system you have linked with will POST to that address when a new commit is made, thus enabling continuous deployment. If you want to disable the continuous feed, you need to do this in the respective system. For example, in Bitbucket, you would go to the repository's settings, select Services, and change or remove the POST URL present among your services integration details.*

Publishing from Team Foundation Service

The flagship of collaboration for teams that develop on the Microsoft stack, Team Foundation Server has really broadened its horizons. Once a tool often feared and misunderstood, TFS relied heavily on a thorough understanding of the "Visual Studio way" and a persistent connection to a central server. Today, Team Foundation Server has re-manifested itself in other incarnations that support distributed source control, and it can be served up in web-sized doses that please developers of all walks.

The incarnation you'll be working from here is Team Foundation Service, accessible at tfs.visualstudio.com, and it works a little differently than the other source control services you have examined in this chapter. Rather than pull in source code and build the solution, TFS publishes the build to the connected Windows Azure Web Site when a check-in builds successfully. In addition, you can integrate a whole host of other options into the build process as well, giving you quite a bit of control and flexibility over how your deployments are built and managed.

Here are the steps you must perform to wire up your solution to TFS and ultimately enable publishing from Team Foundation Service:

1. Log into TFS and create a new Team Project using the default settings. For process template choose "Microsoft Visual Studio Scrum" and select "Team Foundation Version Control" for version control.

2. Open the Simple Site solution in Visual Studio 2012. This solution is located in the Basic Site Publishing Files folder in the code download.

3. Connect to the Team Project you created in TFS. Select Team ⇨ Connect to Team Foundation Server from the Visual Studio menu. Follow any authentication prompts and configure your connection to your TFS server, if required. Select your Team Project and click Connect.

4. Add the solution to the Team Project. From Solution Explorer, right-click on your solution and select Add Solution to Source Control, then click OK.

5. Check your solution in. From Solution Explorer, right-click on your solution and select Check In..., and then click the Check In button on the Pending Changes panel.

Your solution is now wired to automatically build whenever you check in files, as a default Continuous Deployment build configuration will be added to your Team Project.

The next step is to associate your Windows Azure Web Site to this build server through the Azure portal:

1. Create a new website using the Quick Create template. You can create a new website from anywhere in the portal by clicking the New link in the command bar.

2. From the website dashboard, click the link to "Set up deployment from source control." This is located under the Quick Glance area of the dashboard.

3. Enter your Team Foundation Service URL, which you can find on the Account Home page of TFS under the Getting Started title. You will be prompted to allow the link from TFS to Azure, which you should accept.

4. Select the project you want to associate to the website. After authenticating and completing the link, the Azure portal loads the list of projects associated with your URL and presents them in a dropdown. Choose your project and click the checkmark to confirm your selections.

You'll have to wait a moment or two while Azure completes the marriage between your website and the TFS project, but you should see a confirmation at the end of the process as shown in Figure 3-4.

FIGURE 3-4

The next step is to trigger a build, which in turn pushes deployment out to your site. Almost there!

1. In Visual Studio, open `Index.cshtml`. It is located under the Views\Home folder of the project.

2. Change the page's ‹H2› tag to the following:

   ```
   <h2>Phone Book</h2>
   ```

3. Check in your changes. You can right-click on the `Index.cshtml` file in Solution Explorer and select "Check in," or navigate to your Team Explorer home page and select the Pending Changes link to do this.

This check-in activates the continuous integration trigger on your build configuration and will queue a build in TFS. When the build completes successfully, you'll see the deployment process kick off from the Deployments tab of your website in the Azure portal, shown in Figure 3-5. At this point, it is important to note that step 3 is all you need to do going forward to update your website.

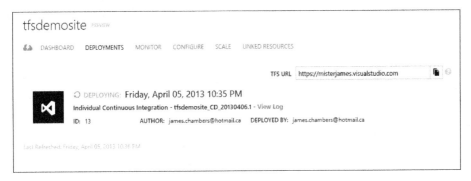

FIGURE 3-5

When the deployment is completed, Azure switches over to the new code base and your site is immediately live. You can view the results of your handiwork by clicking the Browse button in the command bar.

MANAGING PREVIOUSLY DEPLOYED RELEASES

There's nothing worse than pushing a chunk of code out that introduces new problems, especially when you were trying to fix something in the first place! (Of course, this never happens to you because you all write tests, right?) Over the years you've likely come up with processes to make backups of your websites, or you check installers into your versioning control system to ensure that you could easily roll back if a deployment goes sideways on you. These were previously legitimate processes, but in today's world of continuous integration and continuous deployment these manual methods of versioning tend to be difficult to use and require constant effort to maintain.

Or consider the situation in which you haven't yet managed to work your project into SAAS nirvana, and you are managing several sites for multiple clients that are potentially running on different versions of your code base. You're notified of a problem and you need to write unit or acceptance tests to identify which versions are affected, but your test and staging environments are matched to the latest version of the code base. How will you test each of the versions?

The concept of managed deployments makes this task trivial, as all previously deployed versions of your site remain persistent in your site's dashboard. Better still, the deployments are available through the command-line interface, so they're also scriptable, perfect for our world of continuous integration and deployment. You'll get a chance to see this in action in Chapter 4, "Managing Windows Azure Web Sites from the Console."

NOTE *Binding your website to a source control provider is not a permanent operation, and you can disconnect from source control rather easily from the Windows Azure portal. Keep in mind, however, that the list of previous deployments will be discarded when you complete the disconnection. This is one of the caveats you'll face if you choose to switch your back-end link to source control.*

The continuous deployment approach through source control systems is a fairly pleasant experience in its own right. Each deployment created from your check-in is persisted in the portal for each of your websites in Azure. You can access the complete list, a sample of which is shown in Figure 3-6, by navigating to the Deployments tab on any site configured for source control integration.

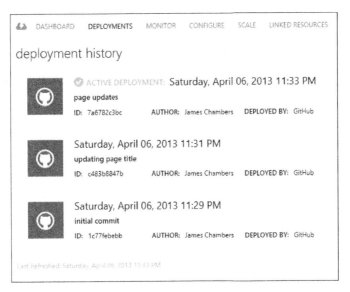

FIGURE 3-6

Let's have a closer look at the information available for each deployment. Hover over any deployment to see an arrow in the top right corner that, when clicked, reveals details for the selected deployment, such as the active deployment shown in Figure 3-7.

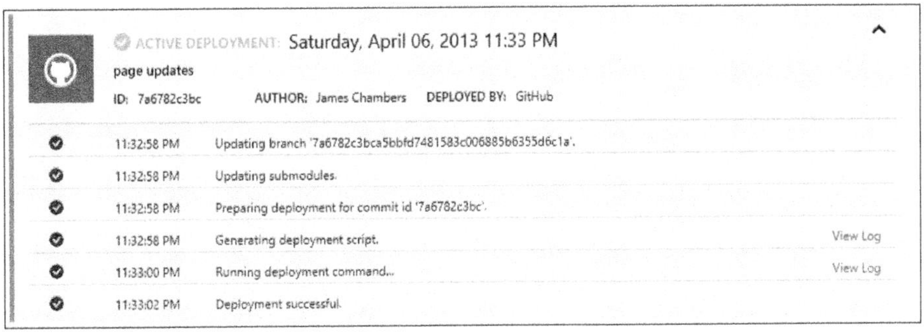

FIGURE 3-7

Any previous deployment you've created can easily be redeployed from this list. Simply click on the deployment you would like to re-instate, then choose the Redeploy command from the command bar. You will be prompted for confirmation, but then the operation only takes seconds and your site will be running on an older version of your code base.

SUMMARY

Your familiarity with various source control systems puts you in an enviable position in the marketplace, and the ability to apply your knowledge to the cloud is an additional benefit. Using your skills with different versioning platforms, you have seen how simple it can be to tie a website hosted in Windows Azure back to a source control system. The process is further enhanced through automated builds and deployments following a successful check in through the supported providers.

Building on what you've learned about creating and managing sites in the previous chapters, you can now review previous deployments of your project and move between versions through the Windows Azure portal via your website's dashboard. With a handle on these soft skills, you'll next learn to manipulate Windows Azure Web Sites through the command-line interface (CLI).

4 Managing Windows Azure Web Sites from the Console

IN THIS CHAPTER:

➤ Tuning up your system to execute the Azure cmdlets

➤ Managing site state and application settings

➤ Getting comfortable with building more complex scripts

She checks her watch; there are only minutes to spare. It's dark, and it's getting darker. The guards are closing in, but their weapons are the least of her worries. The clock seems to run faster and faster, and it won't be long until the good guys, nay, the whole planet, will have all but run out of time. The music crescendos as time appears certain to favor the antagonists, and the only hope left for all of humanity is to connect to a distant satellite and override the nuclear launch control codes. And what does our heroine do? Browse to a website? Open Visual Studio? No! She opens a command-line shell!

There is something uber-geeky and smart-looking about anyone who seems to have good control of their systems from a command line. If you're a touch typist and know your command set well, you can move very quickly inside of a shell and, better yet, write scripts to help automate anything that exposes a compatible interface.

Your typical day at the office may not be quite as compelling as the heroine above, but there are many practical applications for having a handle on what you're able to do and knowing the fastest way to do it. With Azure, it may very well be from within PowerShell, and the Windows Azure cmdlets (pronounced "command-lets") are the way to get there.

In addition, if you don't use PowerShell but instead prefer a different shell or operating system altogether, all the features described in this chapter are available to you in the Azure Cross-Platform CLI tools with minor syntax changes here and there. Use what you're comfortable using!

PREPARING YOUR ENVIRONMENT

If you haven't used any third-party external cmdlets on your system you need to first grant the proper permissions for scripts to execute in PowerShell. The default policy is the most secure, allowing only individual commands to run, but no scripts and certainly no unsigned scripts or configuration files.

The Windows Azure cmdlets are signed and thus require the execution policy called RemoteSigned. This permission level allows you to write your own scripts and will only run scripts and configuration files downloaded from the Internet that are digitally signed. Here's how to do that:

1. Open PowerShell as an administrator by right-clicking on the PowerShell icon and selecting Run as Administrator if you are running in least privilege mode. You won't always need to run as admin, but it is required for setting the execution policy.

2. Set the execution policy to RemoteSigned. Type the following command:

    ```
    Set-ExecutionPolicy RemoteSigned
    ```

You can close PowerShell at this point and your execution policy settings will be saved for future sessions, even when running as a standard user.

Next, it's time to download the cmdlet installer and get them on your machine:

1. Navigate to `http://go.microsoft.com/?linkid=9811175&clcid=0x409` in your web browser.

2. Select the download for Windows Azure PowerShell.

3. When the download is complete, run the installer.

The installer is just a quick download of less than 100KB that launches the Web Platform Installer with the Windows Azure PowerShell cmdlets selected for download. You will encounter a licensing agreement that, while you're free to consent or not as you wish, only after acceptance will the installation finish successfully. Congratulations! You're now one step closer to saving the world from thermonuclear warfare or, more likely, scripting some Windows Azure operations.

NOTE   *The Web Platform Installer (WebPI) should be your preferred method of download and installation, if given the option when working with web development tools and Windows Azure tools in particular. Most applications served through WebPI have the capability to check for compatibility, install dependencies, and generally help you avoid any headaches getting your tools to run. Once installed, related downloads, applications, and tooling are often recommended to complement your installation.*

CONFIGURING YOUR ACCOUNT

Even if you only work with one Windows Azure subscription throughout the course of your daily responsibilities, the PowerShell scripts need to have correct information on hand in order to manage your subscription and its assets. To provide this information you can download a single file representing the authority to manipulate your websites and any other Windows Azure pieces you've created, installing it once.

The file you'll download is simply an XML document similar to the following:

```xml
<?xml version="1.0" encoding="utf-8"?>
<PublishData>
  <PublishProfile
    PublishMethod="AzureServiceManagementAPI"
    Url="https://management.core.windows.net/"
    ManagementCertificate="WsVKB6VrZtmwG6...OFtFwrUk5g==">
    <Subscription
      Id="111111a1-b22b-333c3-d444-e5e555ee55e5"
      Name="Subscription Name" />
  </PublishProfile>
</PublishData>
```

This document contains a root `PublishData` node. And contained within is the `PublishProfile` node, with its attributes — `PublishMethod`, `Url`, and `ManagementCertificate` — along with all of the subscriptions you have tied to your Microsoft Account, including those subscriptions delegated to you by others. The subscription IDs and names are stored with your management certificate when you import the file. You can import multiple files and easily switch between subscriptions, and the Windows Azure PowerShell cmdlets will keep track of them for you behind the scenes.

NOTE *Your settings file contains critical publishing information and your account management certificate. It is all that anyone needs to be able to command your Windows Azure properties. After downloading this file, be sure to store it in a secure location or to delete it after you have imported the file to the Windows Azure PowerShell tools.*

Windows Azure keeps track of all the management certificates that are part of the publishing profiles that have been downloaded for your account. As shown in Figure 4-1, the list of management certificates is viewable from the Settings menu item in the portal. Note that issued certificates do expire, so you'll have to keep that in mind if you intend to use the PowerShell cmdlets as part of an automated process.

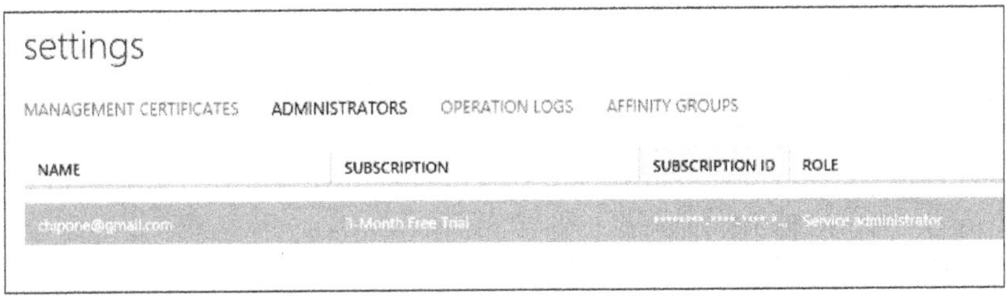

settings

MANAGEMENT CERTIFICATES	ADMINISTRATORS	OPERATION LOGS	AFFINITY GROUPS	
NAME	SUBSCRIPTION		SUBSCRIPTION ID	ROLE
chipone@gmail.com	3-Month Free Trial		********-****-****-*	Service administrator

FIGURE 4-1

Downloading Your Publishing Profile

While the mechanics of downloading your profile is a straightforward operation, the process is a little more difficult if you have multiple subscriptions to work with. The basic flow is as follows:

1.   Open a PowerShell console.

2.   Type the following command:

     ```
     Get-AzurePublishSettingsFile
     ```

3.   Sign into your Windows Azure account, if prompted, in the browser page that was opened in your default browser.

4.   Save the file to a known location.

Step number 3 that can become a little convoluted, especially if you have saved your credentials in your browser or you're using an operating system (such as Windows 8) that has the ability to pass on the credentials of the currently signed-in user account through Internet Explorer. To get around this, you can take advantage of the fact that Windows will try to open the requested link in an existing browser session, if available. To sign in using an account other than the cached credentials, you can do the following:

1.   Close any open instances of Internet Explorer. This ensures that the browser you're opening will be the one targeted when you try to download your settings file.

2.   Start InPrivate browsing in Internet Explorer by right-clicking on the Internet Explorer icon and selecting the InPrivate option.

3.   Follow the steps listed in the previous section as described. When you get to step 3, the browser opened in InPrivate mode will not have any cached credentials, thus allowing you to sign in with an alternate account.

NOTE *It's a good idea to save your settings file to a directory that is easy to navigate to from a command line, such as* c:\azure. *Later, when you go to import the settings, you'll save some keystrokes moving around the file system!*

If you want to work with multiple Microsoft Accounts from PowerShell, you can repeat the preceding steps for each account; just remember to close all your open browser windows at the start of each cycle.

Importing Settings

With your settings downloaded you can now import the profile of each account.

1. Open PowerShell.

2. Navigate to the directory where you saved your publishing profiles.

3. Execute the following command:

```
Import-AzurePublishSettingsFile .\your_file_name.publishsettings
```

Remember that you can use tab completion in PowerShell, so if you're in the directory where the file is created, you simply need to press Tab to complete the filename of your publish settings file.

The utility will import the data for you and cache the information in the roaming data folder of your account, located at `C:\Users\%UserProfile%\AppData\Roaming\Windows Azure PowerShell`, where a number of different files are created to store the information:

➤ `Config.json` — A JSON representation of your account information

➤ `DefaultSubscriptionData.xml` — Contains the complete list of imported account profiles

➤ `publishSettings.xml` — The cache used to represent the account currently in context for Windows Azure PowerShell cmdlets

If, for any reason, you want to clear the settings for your Azure accounts in PowerShell, navigate to the preceding directory and delete all the files. This doesn't affect your account, it just removes all the certificates and subscription IDs that are required to publish to your Azure properties from your local computer. You can download and import the settings again at any time.

NOTE *Deleting the files in your roaming folder for Windows Azure PowerShell will not have an immediate effect on any open PowerShell consoles. Some of the settings information is loaded when you start to use the Azure cmdlets, and this information is cached for as long as you leave the console open. You need to restart PowerShell if you want to fully clear the cache.*

Switching between Subscriptions

The first publishing profile that you import will be saved as the default on your machine, but you can switch between different profiles if you know the name. If you have already imported the settings, you can also get the name of the subscription locally, either by examining the import file or from the Windows Azure PowerShell tools themselves. To get the names from a PowerShell console type the following command:

```
Get-AzureSubscription
```

This will return a listing of all the subscriptions that you've imported. For each subscription there is a field in this listing called SubscriptionName. For the purposes of this example, that field contains the value "3-Month Free Trial"; therefore, to switch to that account and start using it in the context of the Azure cmdlets, you need to type the following:

```
Select-AzureSubscription "3-Month Free Trial"
```

Now, any of the scripts that need to use the context of a subscription will operate in the context of this subscription. The cache files will be updated to reflect your current context; and as you use the scripts, other files will be created in this folder. It's interesting to watch this directory as you use the cmdlets to see what the scripts are doing behind the scenes!

MANAGING YOUR SUBSCRIPTION AND WEB SITES

With your publishing profile imported and your default subscription set, you're ready to begin using the cmdlets and flexing your shell might. Go, you superhero, go! Start with a basic command that enables you to see the websites you've already created in your account:

```
Get-AzureWebsite
```

Like many other PowerShell commands, the "naked" get command returns the full list of objects for all of the Azure Web Sites in the current subscription. If you run the same command again and pass in the name of a specific site, the script will return many of the configuration points, site-specific publishing information, and more, as shown in Figure 4-2. Try the same command but pass in the name of a site:

```
Get-AzureWebsite -Name YourSiteName
```

FIGURE 4-2

This is a good script to keep in your back pocket, as it is easy to survey the state of your websites or the properties of a specific site. When using the command as part of a more complex script, you could do more interesting things by filtering and piping the results of the command to other operations. For example, you could restart all your websites that have "acceptancetest" in their name with the following script:

```
Get-AzureWebsite |
    Where-Object { $_.Name -like "*acceptancetest*" } |
    ForEach-Object { Restart-AzureWebsite $_.Name }
```

Therefore, while you're working through the following cmdlets, keep in mind that though their premise is often simple, you can actually work them into more interesting scripts to orchestrate operations of much greater complexity.

NOTE *When you are trying out commands in this section, be aware that Azure hostnames must be unique. If I have already created the site "MyNothingSite," I will have reserved the hostname "mynothingsite.azurewebsites.net" and you, understanding reader, won't be able to reuse it. If you get an error indicating that a site name has been snatched up by a previous Windows Azure Web Site Customer, just pick a new one and keep rolling.*

Creating Sites

Some things are kept cleverly simple. Take, for instance, creating a new Web Site in your Azure portal:

```
New-AzureWebsite MyNothingSite
```

Your site won't do anything, but it will be created for you and left running with the standard "This web site has been successfully created" message on a default page, and you can manage it from PowerShell (or the portal) as you would any other site.

Creating sites from the command line isn't always going to be practical, but you may find reason for it throughout the course of your development adventures; for example, if you need to replicate a Web Site across different regions to improve the overall performance for your users or if you want to perform a Web Site deployment as part of a build process.

Consider the following script, which accepts the full path of a local directory in a GitHub repository. It spins up the website for you in your Azure account, creates a deployment based on your last GitHub check-in, and displays the site in your browser:

```
param(
  [string] $SiteName=[guid]::NewGuid().ToString(),
  [parameter(Mandatory=$true)] [string] $FullPath
)
```

```
# save the current location and switch to the path provided
Push-Location
cd $FullPath

# create the website and store the script result
$createData = New-AzureWebsite $siteName -GitHub

# output the host name of the created website
$createData.HostNames[0]

# switch back to the orginal directory
Pop-Location
Set-Location

# pause for dramatic suspense (...and git deployment)
Start-Sleep 30

# launch the site in a local browser
Show-AzureWebsite $SiteName

Return
```

A word of caution when running the script: The directory indicated by the $FullPath parameter must be a valid GitHub repository. If not, then the script receives an error suggesting that the data at the root level is invalid.

This little bit of code will start to give you an idea of some of the power you have with the PowerShell cmdlets. The script enables you to create a site with a random GUID if you don't pass in the name of a site, so it also outputs the first (and only) hostname of your newly created site. If you want to give it a try, perform the following steps:

1. Open the PowerShell ISE.

2. Save the preceding script into a file called CreateSite.ps1.

3. Navigate to the directory in which the script is located.

4. From the PowerShell console, call the script and pass in the name of a folder with a GitHub repository. You could, for example, use the simple site that you deployed in Chapter 3. Had you saved that repository in a directory called "c:\azure\simplesite" you could execute the script as follows:

```
.\CreateAndLaunchSite.ps1 -FullPath c:\azure\simplesite
```

Controlling Site State

These are the bread-and-butter commands of any web developer. You've likely worked from the command line before to restart IIS, or perhaps you've even used WMI in PowerShell to start, stop, or recycle a website or app pool. To do the same to your Windows Azure Web Sites, you just follow the standard verb-noun syntax of PowerShell and pass in the name of your site. For example, use the following to stop your site:

```
Stop-AzureWebsite YourSiteName
```

To restart it, use this:

```
Start-AzureWebsite YourSiteName
```

Or, if you want to do it all in one fell swoop:

```
Restart-AzureWebsite YourSiteName
```

Here are some suggestions for how you may be able to use these as part of your scripts:

➤ Your site exposes an API and you have a secondary website or application that consumes the API. You want to introduce some instability in the back-end application to test fault tolerance in the consuming application.

➤ You are penny-pinching and want to turn off sites when you reach certain usage levels to avoid charges, and automatically turn them back on when your billing cycle starts anew.

➤ You are testing cold-start (the traditional IIS kind, not the deactivated Azure Web Site kind) performance for your website.

➤ You need to reset the cached values associated with your website.

Removing Sites from Your Account

When you are done with a site, for whatever reason, you can always remove it using the same syntax format and a straightforward command from PowerShell or within a script:

```
Remove-AzureWebsite YourSiteName
```

The Remove-AzureWebsite cmdlet will, by default, give you a confirmation prompt before it carries out the operation. If you wish to suppress this, simply add the –Force parameter like so:

```
Remove-AzureWebsite YourSiteName –Force
```

Confirming Your Account and Site Status

If you've had your Windows Azure Portal open through this last set of exercises, you likely noticed that the portal tends to get a little behind, particularly when you're issuing a higher volume of commands. This is primarily due to caching for performance of the web portal, but it can lead to short-lived discrepancies between the actual state of a particular site or the number of websites active on your account.

At any time, you can fetch a complete listing of all your sites, with a glimpse of the current state, by running the Get-AzureWebsite command. The results will be similar to what is shown in Figure 4-3, where you can see the GUID-named site is in a stopped state.

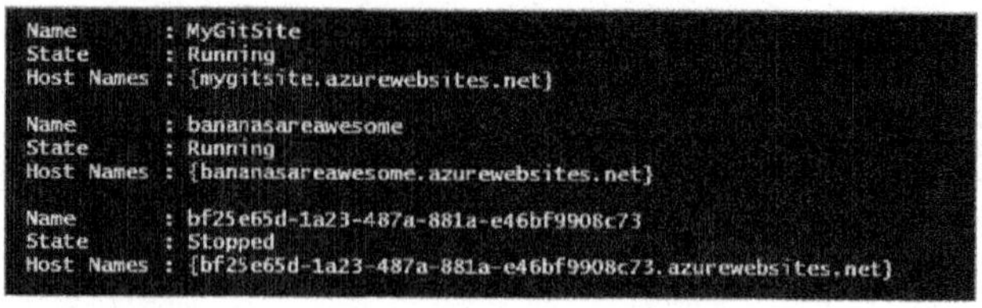

```
Name        : MyGitSite
State       : Running
Host Names  : {mygitsite.azurewebsites.net}

Name        : bananasareawesome
State       : Running
Host Names  : {bananasareawesome.azurewebsites.net}

Name        : bf25e65d-1a23-487a-881a-e46bf9908c73
State       : Stopped
Host Names  : {bf25e65d-1a23-487a-881a-e46bf9908c73.azurewebsites.net}
```

FIGURE 4-3

CONFIGURING YOUR SITE

Chances are pretty good that you'll be using web.config transforms or publishing profiles to bake changes into your configuration as you push to the cloud. But you may find on occasion that modifying its details needs to be done outside of the deployment process. Perhaps you might find a value in your web.config file might be used to determine which part of a script is to be executed. In this section, you learn about the different commands that are available for you to perform basic functionality on the web.config file.

Listing Application Configuration Elements

The Windows Azure Portal provides a clean interface to create, view, and modify your app settings, as shown in Figure 4-4. These values are loaded at start-up and available to your application when it runs. When you fetch the details of your website with the Get-AzureWebsite command, similar to the call illustrated in Figure 4-2, you will only be able to see the names of existing keys, but not the values. Examining the list of keys for the same set of app settings, you might see something similar to the following:

AppSettings   : {good-fruit, best-fruit, better-fruit}

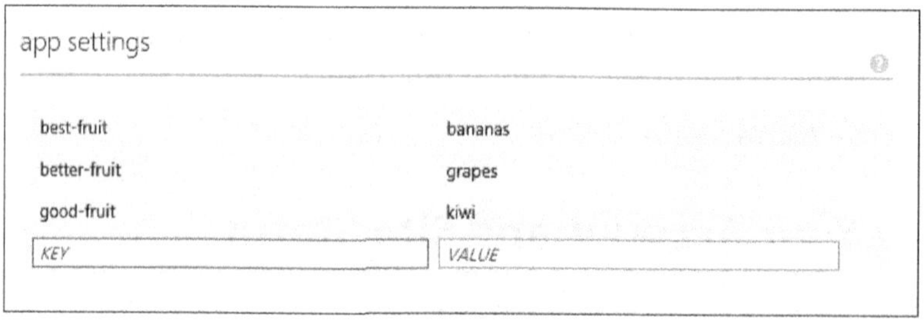

```
app settings                                                                    ⓘ

    best-fruit                        bananas

    better-fruit                      grapes

    good-fruit                        kiwi

    KEY                               VALUE
```

FIGURE4-4

The Get-AzureWebsite command returns an object with properties on it, and the results are displayed in a table of key-value pairs. As you get more comfortable working with PowerShell, you'll notice that this is a common representation of an object, and properties are often condensed and displayed with very little meat on the bone. In other words, if you have a property with a value that is another object, you won't see many of the details.

In the case of our app settings, the property value is another set of key-value pairs. To coerce the values of those keys out of the cmdlet, you need to instead return the property itself. The shorthand version of this command is as follows:

```
(Get-AzureWebsite YourSiteName).AppSettings
```

When I issued this command against my fantastically fruity website, I got the following output:

Name	Value
good-fruit	kiwi
best-fruit	bananas
better-fruit	grapes

Of course, you're in PowerShell, so you're required to do something more interesting, right? The names and values you see here are actually part of a HashTable object, so you can manipulate the collection by getting the enumerator and piping the results into additional commands. The following command sorts the collection of app settings by the value — largest value first — and outputs as part of a string:

```
(Get-AzureWebsite YourSiteName).AppSettings.GetEnumerator() |
    Sort-Object Value -Descending |
    ForEach-Object { Write-Host $_.Key 'is set to' $_.Value }
```

You can use this technique to extract the data you are looking for out of other properties on the object returned from Get-AzureWebste, such as for installed SSL certificates or your site's connection strings.

Adding, Updating, and Deleting Keys

In the preceding section you were working with values that already existed, either from a previous shell session or perhaps as a result of what you configured in the Azure Portal. But what if you wanted to create the app settings from scratch? No problem, but you're going to have to wire up the hashtable by hand in PowerShell first, then pass that object in to the Set-AzureWebsite cmdlet:

```
$settings = @{
  "best-fruit" = "bananas";
  "better-fruit" = "grapes";
  "good-fruit" = "kiwi"
}
Set-AzureWebsite YourWebSite -AppSettings $settings
```

Now the base keys are there, but there is one additional step that still needs to be performed (but was left out of your first go-round); for this example, imagine you had meant to include a property defining the worst fruit but forgot it. The AppSettings property on the Get-AzureWebsite cmdlet result is a hashtable. To add your worst-fruit property, start by getting a reference to the hashtable and then add your new property to the collection. Finally, you would push the resulting set of data back to your site:

```
$settings = (Get-AzureWebsite YourWebSite).AppSettings
$settings.Add("worst-fruit", "tomatoes")
Set-AzureWebsite YourWebSite -AppSettings $settings
```

But what if, in your haste to get that key-value pair up in the cloud, you accidentally added the wrong value (in other words, tomatoes really aren't the worst fruit) and need to rectify the value of your setting. You don't want to modify any of the previous values, so again you start by grabbing your settings from the portal, then adjust the value in the hashtable before shipping it back up into the sky.

```
$settings = (Get-AzureWebsite YourWebSite).AppSettings
$settings.Set_Item("worst-fruit", "dried prunes")
Set-AzureWebsite YourWebSite -AppSettings $settings
```

While the property types vary on the different objects, this fetch-update-store pattern is very applicable to other settings as well. If you wanted to update a specific connection string you would do the following:

1. Fetch the list of connection strings on your site.

2. Update the connection string you need to modify in the collection.

3. Push the collection of connection strings back up to the site.

To translate that back into PowerShell, you might end up with something like this:

```
# fetch the current collection of strings
$connectionStrings = (Get-AzureWebsite YourWebSite).ConnectionStrings
# select the specific string you're updating
$connectionStrings |
    Where-Object { $_.Name -eq "DefaultConnection" } |
    ForEach-Object { $_.ConnectionString = "Details-Go-Here" }

# store the details back in the cloud
Set-AzureWebsite YourWebSite -ConnectionStrings $connectionStrings
```

If you ever need to remove a setting or connection string from the site, you would follow a similar set of steps, downloading the details, modifying the collection, and then pushing it back to your account. For example, consider the following script, which would remove the connection string named ExtraConnection from the config file.

```
$connectionStrings = (Get-AzureWebsite YourWebSite).ConnectionStrings
$connectionStrings |
    Where-Object { $_.Name -eq "ExtraConnection" } |
    ForEach-Object { $_.Remove }

Set-AzureWebsite YourWebSite -ConnectionStrings $connectionStrings
```

SUMMARY

For most purposes you'll find that working in the Windows Azure Management Portal is a pleasant experience. You will be able to manage the bulk of your work without much grief, and nearly all of the requisite functionality will only be a click away.

When it comes time to automate some of that functionality, you're now better equipped to tackle the chore and create reusable scripts to help with initial creation and deployment, configuration, and state management. You've explored the basic commands and know how to control various aspects of your site through the Windows Azure PowerShell cmdlets, updating existing values or removing them from your website.

5 Working with Other Flavors of Windows Azure Web Sites

The prestige is a pivotal point in a magic act when the magician takes an already impressive trick to the next level and shows the audience something they've never seen. The folks working on the Windows Azure team have had plenty of wins over the last year: a newly designed interface that makes configuration, deployment, and scaling more accessible; streamlined publishing options; and improved CLI integration, to name only a few. As Microsoft continues to improve upon its cloud efforts, Windows Azure is in many ways becoming the company's "prestige."

If you're from outside the .NET camp, you've likely been wondering how some of the things in the peripheral view of the portal come into play in your development space; and if you're a .NET developer (and you have been paying attention to the Windows Azure world), you might have seen hints that Azure will contain functionality that is intended for people outside of the Microsoft world.

And you'd be correct.

It turns out that, when it comes to Windows Azure, the "dot-netters" of the world aren't the only ones who get to have fun. Azure has embraced the open source community and made many non-Microsoft technologies feel right at home when running on Windows Azure, even from within alternative and competing development environments.

If you're crossing over from another community, this is the chapter for you, replete with the information you need to bring your site to the cloud. If you're a regular Visual Studio user, this chapter will give you a glimpse of how things roll for your development brothers and sisters with a different gait to their walk.

EXPLORING APPS IN THE WEB SITE GALLERY

You'll find a growing number of templates in the Gallery for Windows Azure Web Sites, handily categorized. The list of projects you can use to kick-start your own is diverse and offers everything from bare-bones starter sites to rich applications with dynamic content.

Here is a sampling of the current categories at the time of writing that you'll find as you create an app-based site in the portal:

➤ **App Frameworks** — Foundations for application development backed by active communities and great documentation

➤ **Blogs** — The fundamentals you need to create and host a blog site on Windows Azure

➤ **CMS** — Going beyond a straight blog, complete management systems to compose sites with multiple authors and varying levels of extensibility

➤ **E-Commerce** — Offers a quick way to implement shopping cart functionality and content pages with an eye to payment gateways and social-enabled commerce

➤ **Forums** — Simple starting points to enable users to interact with each other on your website

➤ **Galleries** — Offers comprehensive CMS capabilities as well as transcoding and thumbnailing services to share media and its metadata on the web

➤ **Templates** — From boilerplate, no-frills documents to turnkey multi-page sites that include membership in a variety of languages

➤ **Wiki** — Enables you to easily add crowd-sourced documentation in the style of several well-known sites

Pick your language, pick your open-source project, or pick your empty document in a language of your choice and get going. The Azure portal provides a wizard-style interface to select a template; and if there are additional steps to perform, such as associating a database, it will help you through those steps as well.

SELECTING A TEMPLATE

The list of web apps available continues to grow, and the projects in the list are updated on a regular basis. When you add a new web app from the Gallery, the portal displays a great template browser, illustrated in Figure 5-1, that enables you to read an overview of any of the templates.

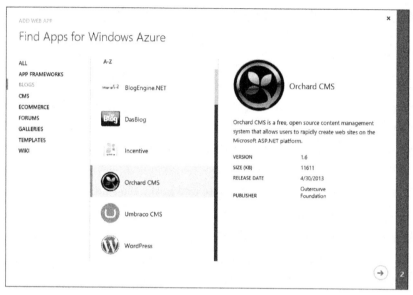

FIGURE 5-1

At the time of writing, there were nearly three dozen templates in this expanding list, all of which provide a good opportunity for exploring a project you haven't worked with previously, or perhaps one that you haven't revisited in quite some time. Even if you have only a trial membership or you're registered for pay-as-you-go service, Windows Azure Web Sites gives you 10 free websites so that you can easily experiment with the ones you would like to learn more about. The following sections demonstrate how you can hop on board with a popular open source forum.

Sample Implementation and Publishing Walk-Through — phpBB

The Internet has long been adorned with bulletin boards, which shifted from dial-in services to widely available conversational "water coolers" throughout the 1990s to a point where now it's odd to see a community-facing site that doesn't include some kind of social aspect. While other social networking sites have largely swallowed up forum users and would-be forum users, there is still a place on the web for subject-focused conversations, particularly if you need to moderate the content yourself.

For more than 12 years, the open source phpBB forum has been available for anyone to use on their domain to provide chatter space for their users. Its comprehensive administrative control panel, shown in Figure 5-2, is revered for its flexibility and adaptability to meet the needs of many sites. It's no wonder that hundreds of thousands of installations have been served up to millions of daily users, making phpBB the most widely used open source forum software on the web.

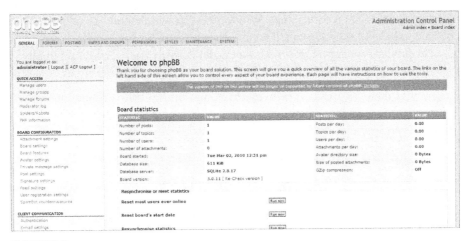

FIGURE 5-2

Found under the Forums category in the Gallery, you can easily create a site in Windows Azure Web Sites that features the phpBB software — and based on my personal experience, this is far easier to do now than it was 12 years ago!

CREATING THE SITE

As with every website on the Internet, you're going to need to carve out a bit of cyberspace for your bulletin board. This is done through the portal, as it has been in previous chapters, where Windows Azure Web Sites takes care of setting aside disk space, registering your subdomain, and creating the appropriate web server mappings:

1. Open your Azure portal by navigating to http://manage.windowsazure.com/ in your web browser and sign in with your credentials.

2. To create a new website, click New in the command bar.

3. Select phpBB from the Gallery. It is easier to find the phpBB template in the list of available apps if you limit your selection to the Forums category.

4. Name your site and configure database access. You can pick any unique name that is not in use on azurewebsites.net, and choose to configure an existing database server or create a new one. Take note of your server name and your database name, and choose a username and password you'll be able to remember, as you will need them later.

5. Confirm your database selection, or complete the information to create a new server and database. If you've chosen an existing server instance, you may need to specify the administrative username and password you used when you created the server (it depends on the type of database server that you're connecting to); otherwise, simply name the database and create a new user.

When you've completed the preceding steps, Windows Azure will happily go off and provision the assets needed to bake the site for you. It creates the site, deploys the codebase, optionally provisions a new database server for you, adds a new database to your server, and finally creates a link between your database and your website for easier management of resources down the road.

When the server has done its duties, it returns a message similar to the following in the notifications pane in the command bar:

The deployment of web site "your_site" succeeded. View the connection information on the Configure page. To set up the application now, click Setup.

Here, you can click the Setup link to begin the process of going live with your site.

Configuring the Board

Once the template is applied and your site is spun up, there are still a few more steps to get it running like the one in Figure 5-3. The one-time configuration provided by phpBB walks you through these steps quite easily. Follow the onscreen prompts to complete your setup with the database settings you captured in the previous section. If you did not save or write down your database settings, you can get them with a little help from the website dashboard in the portal, where you'll find the View Connection Strings link under the Quick Glance section:

1. Start the configuration process on the forum. You can either click the Setup link mentioned in the previous section or browse to your site directly in a web browser. Without an active configuration in place, phpBB assumes that the first person accessing the site is the owner and initial administrator.

2. Click the Install tab. Because you are creating a new forum, you'll follow the script to get a new instance running. When you install new versions, you will be able to upgrade them in place through this installation process from the Convert tab.

3. Click "Proceed to next step" on the welcome screen. There is a bit of text there spelling out the requirements, but your database information and everything else you need from a technical perspective is provided through Azure.

4. Click Start Install from the requirements overview. You might need to scroll down to see the button. Although your site will run without modification, it may be interesting for you to review the checks that are done and read some warnings about features you'll have to install for complete functionality.

5. Enter your database information and click "Proceed to next step"; and after a successful connection to the database, click "Proceed to next step" again. Be sure to specify the MSSQL Server 2005+ [Native] option for the database type. Enter your server hostname, which will be something similar to "g4si46f1c9.database.windows.net," and fill in your database name and credentials. These are the details you recorded in step 4 from the previous section. You can leave the port number blank, and the prefix can be left as the default value of phpbb_.

6. Choose an administrative username and set your credentials. You will also need to provide an e-mail address.

7. Accept the administrator details, then click through the confirmations and options accepting the defaults. You can leave all the default values and complete the installation by continuing to click the "Proceed to next step" buttons on each of the subsequent pages until the final confirmation.

8. Now that you have completed the installation process, the next step is to delete the install folder so that the site will begin to function as designed. The last page of the wizard has several delete links; you can click any one of them.

Your site (a sample of which is shown in Figure 5-3), is now running and you can start posting or inviting folks to sign up.

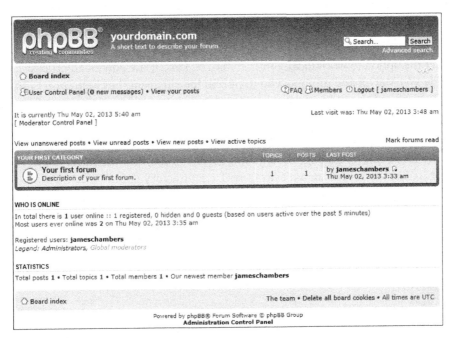

FIGURE 5-3

Working Locally with Project Files

The default site looks great and works fine, but don't you want to customize it, just a little? Of course you do, web warrior! In Chapter 2 you had a chance to work through several methods for pushing a site to the cloud. Now, you'll use one of those methods — WebMatrix — to pull the contents of the site down locally and work from your machine.

There is more to a website than just a file, however, and you'll need to get the database down and onto your system as well. In addition, don't forget that this is a PHP site, so you will have to configure your machine to run PHP. The easiest way to get the job done and get the site up and running locally is actually through the Windows Azure portal.

When you navigate to your site's dashboard, recall that there is a WebMatrix button in the command bar of the portal. Clicking this button not only enables you to open your site in WebMatrix, but also pulls down any other dependencies you need to run the site locally. You can do that now, and prepare to edit the site footer, where you'll let everyone know about your newfound cloud skills:

1. Click the WebMatrix icon in the command bar. You'll need to be logged in to your Windows Azure Portal. Either select the site from the list of items in your account or navigate to the site dashboard, where the WebMatrix icon appears.

2. Download any required dependencies to run the site locally. Be sure to review any licensing agreements and then proceed to install any additional required components to give yourself the richest development experience on your machine.

3. Select the option to work locally in WebMatrix. Part of the download process lands inside WebMatrix and prompts you to pull in the site from the cloud source. This will make a copy of the site and download the database as well as any support files related to phpBB so that you can optionally run the site directly from your machine.

4. Navigate to and open the overall_footer.html file in your project. This file is used to render the footer for all pages on the site outside of the administrative control panel and is located in the styles\prosilver\template directory.

5. Add the following code as the last element in the page_footer div in the file. The page_footer element contains two divs: one attributed with a class called navbar, the other with a class called copyright. You're adding a third div with the same copyright class:

```
<div class="copyright">
    Running on <a href="http://www.windowsazure.com">Windows Azure Web
Sites</a>
    </div>
```

6. Save the contents of the file. This will save your site locally.

You're now ready to sync your site with Windows Azure.

Publishing the Customized Site

With your changes implemented, it's time to see the fruits of your labor live and running from within your website on the cloud. In the case of phpBB there are some additional steps to enable your template, but activating your changes in the forum itself is a separate process from pushing your code. You'll first get the changes out into the cloud using the following steps:

1. Click the Publish button in WebMatrix. This button is displayed in the UI by default when you are editing the local version of the site, but if you have navigated through the software you may need to return to the Home ribbon to see the icon.

2. One of the benefits of the Publish mechanism is that only those files that have been added or modified are sent to the server. At this point, you have the option to review the files that meet these criteria (technically known as the computed difference). For example, if you have altered only the overall_footer.html page, you'll just see one file in the review stage.

3. Confirm your selected files and click Continue to publish to Azure. This will move any selected files — in this case, your newly adorned footer — up to your instance of phpBB in your account.

NOTE *Caching in phpBB introduces new files into your local project if WebMatrix has started running your site locally before you publish. This results in many additional files that look like they need to be uploaded to Windows Azure, but you can ignore any files in the cache directory; these files will be recomputed on the server.*

Next, you need to activate the new version of the template. phpBB creates a cache at startup time that stores a pre-rendered version of files from your template, and the cache needs to be cleared so that the files can be rebuilt. This would happen automatically if you used the built-in editor in phpBB; but when you save the files to disk or publish them through any other means, phpBB doesn't know that it needs to invalidate the cache and rebuild. So you need to help the site out:

1. Navigate to your website. There are many ways to do this, but the easiest might be through the publishing confirmation in WebMatrix. You can type the name of the site directly in the browser, or you can click any of the links in your site's dashboard in the Azure portal.

2. Log in to the site and enter the Administration Control Panel (ACP). There is a link at the bottom of each page to access the administrative area of the site, and you will be prompted to confirm your credentials as you enter.

3. Go to the template management area of the site. To get there, click the Styles tab at the top, then click the Templates link on the left-hand side of the page under the heading Style Components.

4. Clear the site cache. Under the Actions column of the Prosilver template, click the Refresh button and accept the prompt to clear the cache.

With the template updated and the cache cleared, phpBB will recompute your footer on the next visit to the site. As shown in Figure 5-4, the site footer now tells all your visitors where the site is hosted.

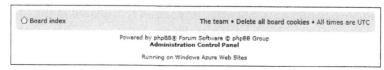

FIGURE 5-4

In this fashion you can add new files, modify graphics such as for the site logo, or modify additional templates and easily move them back into the cloud-hosted site.

Moving beyond the Basic Set Up

The ideas described here have been to simply use the Windows Azure Portal to get the site kick-started and running in the cloud. Using the site template ensures that database resources are linked and critical aspects of your configuration are properly set.

You don't have to edit the template locally, as phpBB offers a way to edit files directly on the site. However, editing locally does have its advantages — namely, a better development experience in a product like WebMatrix, but also the capability to operate under your source control suite of choice. In fact, the Source Control ribbon in WebMatrix enables you to add the project to Team Foundation Server or run Git init on the project directory. In addition, with source control in place, you're able to commit changes to the portal and manage check-in-based deployments, as covered in Chapter 3.

All of these reasons make a compelling argument to use Azure to help spin up a site using a Gallery template but take the steps needed to work on your site locally.

SUMMARY

Open source projects are growing in diversity, popularity, and quality; and they can serve as a great starting point for many projects that you might like to take on. The Gallery in Azure Web Sites enables you to easily browse and select a template from a growing list of categories to begin your efforts, and includes everything from shell projects to fully operational websites.

Whether you've started your site from scratch or elected to use one of the templates provided through the Gallery, you've seen how the cloud can also be very local. Some great tools are provided for those just getting started, and veterans can continue to use their preferred editor to modify their project, update site contents, or add new files and ultimately publish their changes to the cloud.

6 Using Peripheral Features with Windows Azure Web Sites

IN THIS CHAPTER:

➤ Delegating administrative duties for your Windows Azure subscription

➤ Creating links between different types of resources and managing linked resources

➤ Working with Windows Azure SQL Database remotely

There's a certain sort of allure to staying in a hotel. Hotels are like little homes you get to stay in when you can't be in your own, and you don't get into too much trouble if you leave the bathroom messy in the morning. You always come back to a made bed, even if you didn't make it before you stepped out. There's unlimited ice down the hall and you don't have to make the ice cubes. Brilliant.

Not everything you do in your project will deal exclusively with your website. Often you'll have other Windows Azure assets associated with your project and it would be nice to have these easily accessible through the portal. Very few projects lack some kind of database connectivity, and when you have a database involved, you want to be able to get to your data.

So, what do hotels have to do with Windows Azure Web Sites? Maybe more than you think, so stick with me to the end to see where this goes, and don't forget to tip the concierge.

SHARING ADMINISTRATIVE RESPONSIBILITIES

When you check into a hotel you get a key to your room that enables you to come and go as you please. The only other people who can get into your room are people with implied trust — folks that make up part of the cleaning team, or a bellhop that brings your bags to the room for you. If you are expecting a parcel, you can talk to the front desk and arrange to have it brought to your room in your absence by a member of that trusted group.

You also have control over explicit trust. When you want to let someone you trust into your room, you can request a second key to allow them entry and exit privileges as they please, knowing full well that when you are not there, they have the run of the room. They might watch movies, order room service, or even sneak treats from the in-room snack bar. You would be responsible for any charges they incur.

Co-administration in Windows Azure works much the same way. Many hands make light work, and the duties of creating, publishing, monitoring, and maintaining Web Sites certainly qualify as work. It's reasonable to assume that administrators will come across scenarios in which having another set of hands — or several — makes sense for their environment.

Administrators are associated with a subscription and are granted permissions at one of two levels:

➤ **Co-Administrator** — Has permissions to create, modify, and manage Azure assets as well as manage other co-administrators on the subscription; and can create support requests through the Windows Azure support portal that relate to the subscription.

➤ **Service Administrator** — Has the same rights as a co-administrator, but can also view or modify billing information. This is the owner of the subscription and can't be removed by a co-administrator.

There's not much you need to do to allow someone else to jump in and help you with the duties, as shown in Figure 6-1. Adding someone else to your account is as easy as typing that person's e-mail address into the UI, which you can access by following these steps:

1. Open the Settings workspace in the portal.

2. Navigate to the Administrators tab.

3. Click the Add button in the command bar and fill in the details.

ADD A CO-ADMINISTRATOR

Specify a co-administrator for subscriptions

Co-administrators can fully manage the services within a subscription. Enter a valid email address, and then select at least one subscription.

EMAIL ADDRESS

mickeymouse@hotmail.com

SUBSCRIPTION	SUBSCRIPTION ID
☑ My Personal Account	02472315-d3bf-4b18-b7ce-f807d9a25eef

FIGURE 6-1

FIGURE 6-2

The portal contains basic controls for editing related accounts and administrators. Note that anyone who adds you as a co-administrator will appear in your list of administrators, but they are not granted any permissions to your subscriptions by default.

When you have access to more than one subscription in either role, you'll notice subtle changes throughout the Windows Azure portal. When you create a new asset of any kind, when you create support tickets, or when you're managing co-administrators on a subscription or subscriptions to which you've been granted access, you'll see a dropdown list from which you can select the account to which the item is to be associated. In other areas you'll see the subscription noted to help you differentiate which assets belong to which subscription. You'll also see a change in the main menu, as shown in Figure 6-2, enabling you to filter items in any of the lists in the portal by subscription.

The filter also allows you to search your active subscriptions, quite handy if you want to build a business around managing cloud infrastructure for others. If your organization's cloud strategy includes several active subscriptions, this is also a great feature to isolate augmented services or overage charges for billing purposes.

Understanding the Scope of Trust in Co-Administration

Be aware that trust is extended to you only while you exist as an administrator on the other person's account. This is, of course, reciprocal, but there are implications on your end. Returning to the hotel analogy, if you've been given someone else's room key and you put all your stuff in their room, you are accepting the fact that if they tell the front desk to revoke your key you're not getting your belongings back that easily.

The same principle applies to items you create and contribute to in Windows Azure:

➤ **Sites created under someone else's subscription become their property**. It doesn't matter if you create all the assets, architect the data design, write every single line of code, and are the only person who has ever published to the site; if you create a website under their account, it belongs to them as far as Windows Azure is concerned.

➤ **There is no way to move a site from one subscription to another**. I call this the "Vegas" clause, because a website created on a subscription stays on a subscription. You can't port an asset from one subscription to another without opening a support ticket. Beyond the scope of shared administration, this is true even if you own both subscriptions.

➤ **Access to sensitive data is shared between administrators on the account**. There is currently no way to grant someone publishing and scaling permissions but restrict them from other aspects of the administrative portal. If you have permission to access the dashboard of a Windows Azure Web Site, you can see the database connection strings and linked resources, reset publishing credentials, or view log files.

➤ **You have permission to affect permissions**. Pay attention to the permissions you are administering and be aware that if you remove your own permissions you won't be able to add yourself back. Be cognizant of the changes you are making so that you don't inadvertently grant undue access to others' subscriptions.

While these are good cautions to keep in mind, they are not inherently bad things nor reasons to avoid co-administrative duties. You have other ways to provide and restrict access and you don't have to share your subscription information with others if and when it's not appropriate.

Avoiding Shared Administration

There are two scenarios in which you'll likely need a way to restrict access to either your subscription or a particular site. Administration is an on/off switch with no middle ground and yet in some situations you'll want to have someone help with a site (monitoring, scaling, database, or other linked resource management) or publish to that site. Said another way, you have to decide whether you want to give someone a room key or just have them leave your package at the front desk. You have two solid options to isolate the site itself or restrict the developer to administering only a specific site:

➤ **You manage several Windows Azure projects, sites and assets, but want to share administrative duties on one of them**. This scenario can be managed by creating multiple subscriptions. Fees on Azure are accrued based on usage and overages tied to specific properties. There are no costs to holding multiple subscriptions, and by creating a subscription for a single project you can easily add and remove other administrators without granting them access to all the items in your account. In the hotel analogy this is the same as giving a trusted person a key to only the room that you want to let them into.

➤ **You want to maintain administrative control of the site but grant publishing access to other project contributors**. This is actually something that can be handled outside of Windows Azure Web Sites. Configure your site for automated deployments from source control as demonstrated in Chapter 3, and then grant access to your repositories as required. Working in distributed source control systems such as TFS, GitHub, or Mercurial, you can further restrict access by using a fork/pull request model, which I have found to be a great solution for open-source projects. Your source control system becomes the bellhop, only granting access to the bits that you approve of through a trusted source.

The model you choose will obviously be based on the level of trust that you have in working with the team or individual with whom you are sharing the responsibilities; and remember that you can always start with the bellhop and upgrade to the room key if it makes sense in your context, keeping in mind the implications of sharing your subscription with other administrators noted earlier.

MANAGING YOUR LINKED RESOURCES

Many hotels offer a great option for traveling families: two side-by-side rooms — one for the parents, one for the kids — with a door that connects them. If the children are up late misbehaving, you don't have to skirt out into the hallway to settle them back down. Both rooms are fully functional in their own right, and the door between the two isn't always needed. You can, in fact, enter either room from the hallway even if the in-room passage is locked or not there at all.

Linked resources in Windows Azure are much the same. No technological changes are made to either of the assets when you create a link, and deleting one item or removing a link between them doesn't change the function of the other. The assets you have associated will appear under the Linked Resources tab on your website dashboard, as shown in Figure 6-3. When you create a link you're simply making it easier for yourself to navigate between them or to more easily scale and monitor the resources that are being used.

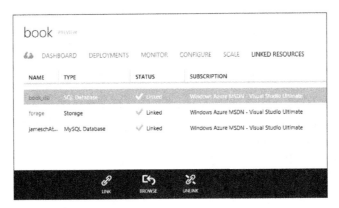

FIGURE 6-3

If, for example, you are going to use Windows Azure SQL Database with your website, you can create a link to the database that enables you to easily navigate to the database dashboard from the website. The connection string for the database, which you'll still need to wire into your project, appears on the website's dashboard. While Windows Azure SQL Database instances are managed in a separate yet similar interface, you can effortlessly traverse the cloud and into the Database workspace simply by clicking the name of the database from the linked resources list.

> **NOTE** *Currently, the only assets you can add as linked resources are Windows Azure SQL Databases, MySQL databases, and Windows Azure storage accounts. I suspect that as the app platform matures, you will see additional integration points. For now, most third-party services can be administered from the Add-ons workspace, where relevant links are added to the Azure portal command bar as required.*

Note in Figure 6-3 that not all links can be used for navigation. Azure properties, such as Windows Azure Storage accounts and Windows Azure SQL Databases, have connected or integrated interfaces into the Windows Azure Management portal, and an HTML link allows you to click through to those interfaces. A MySQL database hosted with a third-party provider does not share the same facilities. In this case, you create a separate login for the external resource and administer it through the provider's own interface (for MySQL the default provider is ClearDB).

There are currently three ways you can create linked resources for your website in the Windows Azure portal:

➤ **When you create your website** — Creating a new "custom site" or choosing to create a new Web Site through one of the templates in the gallery may link one or more resources to your site. The most common will be a database.

➤ **Through the Linked Resources listing on your Web Site dashboard** — From the dashboard you can choose to add links to new databases and storage accounts, or you can create links to existing Windows Azure assets.

➤ **From the Windows Azure Add-on store** — Some services can be added first through the store, then later added as a linked resource to your site. For those that can't be linked, you can still manage the add-on from the Add-ons workspace in the portal.

Don't spend too much time worrying about a particular service, storage account, or add-on not being available as a linkable resource. Although links can be convenient, they only serve as a convenience in the portal and don't automatically integrate the resource into your project; you still need to do the heavy lifting.

WORKING WITH WINDOWS AZURE SQL DATABASES REMOTELY

You're not always going to be in the portal; and quite frankly, the portal interface won't always be the best tool for the job. Databases are a critical part of today's website development process, and developers on the .NET stack are likely going to favor some flavor of MS SQL. When you're building your application with the goal of targeting cloud deployment, Windows Azure SQL Database will probably be part of your development strategy, and working locally affords more features than the portal version can provide.

You will have to make some compromises to adopt the Azure version of SQL, but compromises can be positive things too. What you give up is mostly related to physical management, such as file groups, initial provisioning, and limitations to the backup/restore process. The gains, on the other hand, can be quite significant when you consider the high-availability model of cloud infrastructure, simplified management, and scalability, which enables growth as your business grows.

Ultimately, the goal here is to make a connection from Microsoft SQL Server Management Studio (SSMS), and you will need to use version 2008 R2 or greater to do so. These tools can be downloaded free from Microsoft at `www.microsoft.com/en-us/sqlserver/default.aspx` and follow the links for the Express Edition if you don't already have the tools installed.

Opening the Firewall

There is a high-security model in Windows Azure that allows connectivity only between other Windows Azure assets in your account, and this model extends to Windows Azure SQL Database. You'll need to poke a hole in the firewall and allow your IP address or a range of IP addresses if you want to access the database remotely.

Granting access to your IP address is typically a simple 19-step process requiring approvals from fewer than a dozen folks in your organization — except not on Windows Azure! The process is actually quite straightforward, and you have a couple of options to execute, the first being through the Windows Azure Management portal itself:

1. Navigate to the dashboard of the database in question. The easiest way to do this is through the linked resources of your website, but you can also find it in the database workspace.

2. Click "Manage allowed IP addresses." You can find the link under the Quick Glance section on the database dashboard.

3. Confirm the current address to add to the list of allowed IP addresses. Your current public IP will be displayed in a textbox near the top of the page. Click the confirmation arrow to add your IP to the list, or modify the range of IP addresses (if you're in a dynamically assigned pool of IPs).

4. Save the updates to the configuration of your database. The save icon appears in the command bar after making any changes to this screen.

With the firewall rule in place, you are ready to make your remote connection.

Establishing Remote Connections

The process to connect to a Windows Azure SQL Database is largely the same as that for a traditional SQL instance; you'll need to know the server name and have SQL credentials to log in (Windows Azure SQL Database does not support Windows Authentication). Everything you need can be gained from opening the View Connection Strings link in the Quick Glance section of your website's dashboard, as shown in Figure 6-4. The information is equally available through the dashboard of the database itself.

FIGURE 6-4

With this information in hand you can complete your connection. Again, you can use SSMS for SQL Server 2008 R2 or greater. Though the UI style is updated in 2012, the field names and required fields are the same in both editions. Use the connection information that you gathered from your website dashboard to fill in the Connect to Server dialog displayed in Figure 6-5.

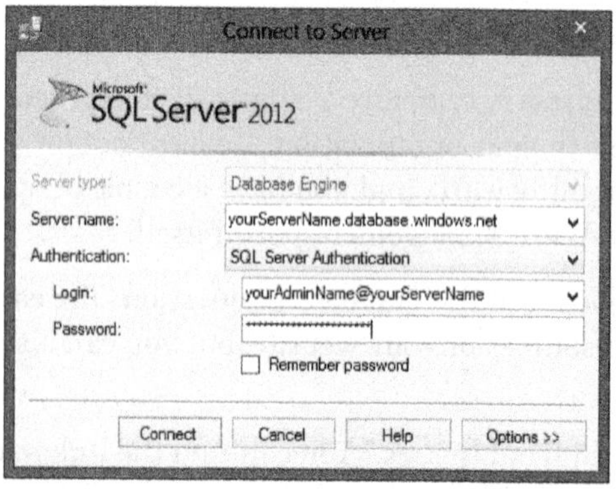

FIGURE 6-5

One of the things that I've run into when moving quickly is specifying a database name instead of the server name, or not following the correct convention for the username when specifying the credentials. For this reason, I've included both the connection string information in Figure 6-4 and the dialog in SSMS in Figure 6-5 so you can see these details as they translate from one to the other.

After you have entered these details, click the Connect button to get your session set up. You'll then be able to use the following features of SSMS with your Windows Azure SQL Database:

➤ Create new databases on the server to which you're connected.

➤ Create queries against any of your existing tables.

➤ Modify the schema of existing objects.

➤ View, manage, or create logins for the server.

➤ Create, manage, and deploy data-tier applications using DACPAC files to define schema and help create migrations.

➤ Create local backups of your SQL Azure Database and restore them on your own instance of SQL Server through the use of BACPAC files.

NOTE *Remember to adhere to your established project guidelines when working with databases remotely. Creating and dropping tables or otherwise modifying schema in SQL Server Management Studio is a trivial exercise but can put your database out of sync with mirrored environments or migrations in Entity Framework, possibly rendering your site inoperable. Remote connections should not be a replacement for proper deployment strategies, but serve as a great utility to query data, build DACPAC files, or troubleshoot erroneous data state.*

There's so much more you can do with Windows Azure SQL Database, including creating and restoring backups through storage accounts, migrating SQL Server Database Engine data out to the cloud through UI or programmatically using BACPAC files, scaling and monitoring, and more. If you will be working with Windows Azure SQL Database on your project, consider reading *Windows Azure Data Storage*, 978-1-118-70883-5 (Wrox, 2013) in this cloud series.

SUMMARY

Sometimes the most important aspects of a project are the ones that live in the wings, the ones that you don't need to touch very often but are critical when you do. At those times, it's important to be able to access them freely and easily, and to call in help when needed.

Windows Azure provides numerous ways to access and manage the assets related to your websites. You can leverage assistance from trusted administrators, share administrative duties, or restrict access as required to help deploy and maintain your website. If the need arises, you can drill into your database using local tools to query, create backups, or modify schema using tools you're likely already aware of as a web developer.

With these administrative tools in your belt, it's time to check out of this chapter and into the next — a world of configuration, transformation, and scale.

7 Scaling, Configuring, and Monitoring Your Site

IN THIS CHAPTER:

➤ Understanding your options for scaling your website for performance

➤ Working with diagnostic logs and troubleshooting your live site

➤ Exploring other aspects of configuration in your Windows Azure Web Site

Not everyone can come up with that one great website idea, the one that sends you to early retirement as droves of Internet citizens sing the praises of your creation. No, the reality is that most of us will be working well past the age of 111100 (in binary); but that's not to say we won't have our ideas, and some may be quite good. What options do you have to host the site?

➤ Buy a single server out of savings and hope that at some point you can scale the hardware while dealing with growth.

➤ Borrow a friend's server and live at his or her mercy when you need changes to DNS, or RAM, or database storage space.

➤ Rent a Virtual Machine (or VM) through a hosting provider and try to figure out how to scale horizontally down the road.

➤ Find a rich aunt or uncle (or angel investor) to pay up-front capital costs to put a bank of servers into commission, then hope for traffic.

While none of these are intrinsically bad ideas — and there are certainly other (possibly better) options out there — they all come with certain restrictions or the potential to make the next family gathering quite uncomfortable. Going back for more capital before you've repaid the initial investment can be tricky, and not all virtualization scenarios are designed to scale in both directions (i.e., when your traffic slows down again).

So how's this for a price point? Free. All Web Sites can start in a free tier of service; then, as the expectations for performance or the success and growth of your idea dictate, you can scale out to meet the needs of your users.

Yes, folks, that's right: Windows Azure Web Sites can make turkey dinner fun again! No more awkward moments after having the money conversation.

USING THE POWER OF THE CLOUD: SCALE

If all my neighbors on the block decided to own just one car for all ten houses, it would be so much less expensive. I would try to pitch this to them if I could come up with a way to plan a precise schedule that would work for everyone, but practical realities prevent a car from appearing exactly where you need it to be for whomever needs it, on demand. Physics is one such reality; but if you could get past those minor details and slice the use of that car up, how would it work? You would get to have a car at a fraction of the cost. If each user returned it with a full tank of gas, those who used more would pay more; and perhaps if there were times when you didn't use it for days, you could pay even less or not at all.

Thankfully, the web is centralized and you don't need to have the server on your premises in order to use it; and unlike a vehicle, a processor operates at billions of cycles per second and is very good at "appearing" exactly where it needs to be in an instant, which makes sharing a server much more attractive than sharing a car. You'll still need to pay for extra scale when you need it (and there's plenty to go around), and your usage will vary from one hour of CPU time per day all the way up to dedicated instances that you don't have to share at all.

Finally, it's worth mentioning that for some features of Windows Azure Web Sites you'll need to step up at least one level from "free" to enable benefits such as using custom domain names for your website and enabling endpoint monitoring.

Understanding Levels of Scale

Regardless of the scaling mode you choose to operate under, you will enjoy similar benefits in all your applications. Your subscription entitles you to free inbound data transfers, free storage transactions from your websites, and a free 20GB MySQL database for the first 12 months of your account.

You can manipulate the scalability of your application from under the General heading on the Configure tab of your Web Site dashboard, as shown in Figure 7-1, where it can be configured to run under one of the following three modes:

➤ **Free** — This is the default scale setting for any newly created site in Windows Azure WebSites. You can host up to 10 free sites in this mode using up to 1GB of storage and a total of 60 minutes of CPU per day, per region. This mode gives you 165MB of outbound traffic per day.

➤ **Shared** — In this mode you can host up to 100 websites per region, consuming up to four hours of CPU cycles, but your bandwidth is a la carte. Don't worry, however, as currently it would cost you only pennies if you had 10GB of traffic. With that kind of volume you'll likely have a business model in place that affords you the $0.60 you'd have to pay!

➤ **Reserved** — When you're configured for reserved mode on your site, you have one or more dedicated CPU instances at your disposal, and your 100 sites will be able to share

10GB of storage. As with the other options, you pay for your outbound traffic at fairly reasonable rates. Reserved pricing is appropriate for high-traffic sites and/or sites with higher processing demands.

FIGURE 7-1

When you move up from the free tier of hosting you are paying for part or all of a CPU and will pay hourly costs associated with that, ranging from $0.02/hour up to $0.40/hour depending on your needs. This puts the price of these configurations in a range of $15/month up to approximately $300/month for the highest available reserved CPU.

NOTE *The charges and allowances here are current at time of writing, but they have changed in the past and are likely to change again. For the most up to date pricing and limits, be sure to visit the overview page on the Azure website at* www.windowsazure .com/en-us/pricing/details/web-sites/.

Changing the mode that your site is running under is as straightforward as clicking the button corresponding to your selection and clicking the save button in the command bar. You will be notified that changes to scale may affect the recurring charges on your subscription and then you have to confirm your intentions if you wish to do so. The changes take only a moment and your site remains running when the switch is made. You will be charged the new rate effective the moment your site flips into the new mode.

Improving Capacity

In shared and reserved mode you can choose to scale "horizontally," meaning you can add additional instances of your website that will automatically be used in load balancing. You can have up to six instances for shared mode and up to 10 instances when you move into a reserved configuration. Figure 7-2 shows a site using 8 of the 10 instances available.

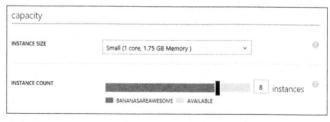

FIGURE 7-2

With reserved mode you can also scale "vertically" by increasing the processing power available to your websites. You can choose from Small (1 core, 1.75GB RAM), Medium (2 cores, 3.5GB RAM), and Large (4 cores, 7GB RAM) instances to help handle your increasing load. Keep in mind that these numbers will affect pricing and act as a multiplier on the base hourly rate used to compute your monthly charges.

Just drag the slider around and use the dropdown box shown in Figure 7-2 to set the overall processing capacity available to your sites. I have to mention here that this is one of the beautiful parts of working with the cloud. I have worked with several network administrators in charge of my server deployments throughout the course of my career, and I can assure you they do not appreciate being dragged around like a slider. Their dropdown boxes are also very difficult to locate.

Scaling Linked Resources

The size of your website proper — in fact, the size of all websites under your subscription — must not exceed the maximum quota for your tier of performance. Therefore, for the free sites you can divide the 1GB of space over 10 sites. For shared and reserved modes, you can split your 100 websites over 1GB or 10GB, respectively. But that's not the only way your site can grow.

As described in Chapter 6, there are two types of manageable linked resources in Windows Azure Web Sites: databases and storage accounts. These are both mechanisms you can use to store data required or generated by your websites, and both carry monthly charges associated with use.

Storage is a linear and decreasing charge as your consumption increases. For basic storage requirements you'll pay as little as $0.07/GB/month of storage space; in a tiered pricing model that drops down to $0.037/GB/month. When you add in features such as geo-redundant capabilities, this can be as much as $0.095/GB/month, dropping to as little as $0.055/GB/month when you hit around 10,000 TB.

For SQL Database you start with two classification options, Web and Business, which opens the door to a number of size selections:

➤ **Web edition** — 1GB or 5GB

➤ **Business edition** — 10/20/30/40/50GB, 100GB, or 150GB

Pricing for SQL Database is also tiered, costing anywhere from $10/GB/month down to $1/GB/month as your required capacity increases. Remember to keep in mind that your database does not include egress charges, so your outbound bandwidth is metered and charged separately.

NOTE *The mode of your site, the number of CPUs you are reserving (and their size), along with databases all play into the actual dollar figure you'll be responsible for when you decide to scale your site. It's impossible to provide exact prices because there are so many variables that can affect how you configure and scale your websites. Before you fire up your formulas in your favorite spreadsheet, the easiest way to approximate what your real costs would be is to visit the Windows Azure Pricing Calculator located at* www.windowsazure.com/en-us/pricing/calculator/.

CONFIGURING AND DOWNLOADING DIAGNOSTIC LOGS

Debugging a live site can be both frustrating and time consuming if you haven't planned ahead. Beyond writing tests to ensure that you capture the obvious and prevent regression errors, you can better equip yourself by using trace statements in your code to provide information on performance or to capture the details of an error message.

Adding a trace message is very straightforward in .NET:

```
Trace.TraceError("Something went terribly wrong...");
```

With that in place throughout your code base, the other thing you'll need to do is to enable logging for your website so that you can capture application tracing. One place you can do this is through the Azure portal, located under the Application Diagnostics header on the Configure tab of your website's dashboard, as shown in Figure 7-3.

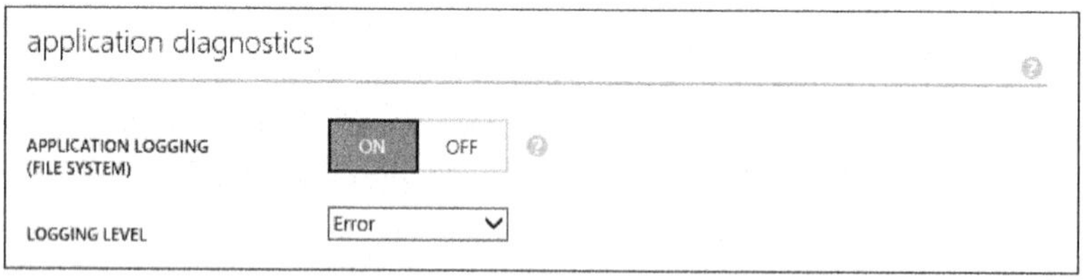

FIGURE 7-3

Enabling this feature will allow application trace logs to be written to the file system of your website and enable streaming for developers who are working on a live issue.

Viewing Trace Information from Visual Studio 2012

Windows Azure Web Sites received a lot of love from the freshly released Windows Azure SDK 2.0. There is a deeper integration with the Web Sites product, and you can manage and configure your site from within Visual Studio. One of the great features is the capability to monitor the trace output from your website's live stream. To enable these features, you need to associate your Azure subscription with Visual Studio; if you haven't done so already, Visual Studio will walk you through the process, prompting you for your credentials and ultimately downloading the configuration required to manage your subscription remotely.

With your subscription configuration imported into Visual Studio, you can now view your Windows Azure Web Sites through the familiar Server Explorer tool window, along with your other Azure properties. When you expand the Windows Azure Web Sites item in the tree, you'll see the list of sites you can manage from your subscription. Right-click on a website to pull up the context menu shown in Figure 7-4.

FIGURE 7-4

Selecting View Streaming Logs in Output Window will reveal the Output window and display the output from Windows Azure Logs for your site. As trace messages accrue on your site, you'll see them appear in your Output window, as illustrated in Figure 7-5.

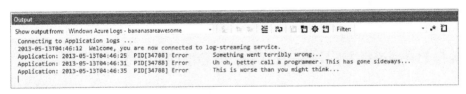

FIGURE 7-5

To stop streaming the trace output, right-click the site again in Server Explorer and select Stop Viewing Logs from the context menu.

Viewing the Logs from the PowerShell Console

PowerShell and the cross-platform CLI tools also get the live streaming love. In PowerShell, the command to view the live stream is as follows:

```
Get-AzureWebsiteLog -Name <yoursite> -Tail
```

Watching the same set of website operations that resulted in the trace messages shown in the previous section, you can see the eerily familiar output in the PowerShell console, as shown in Figure 7-6.

```
PS C:\Windows\system32> Get-AzureWebsiteLog -name bananasareawesome -tail
2013-05-13T04:55:57  Welcome, you are now connected to log-streaming service.
2013-05-13T04:56:01  PID[34788] Error      Something went terribly wrong...
2013-05-13T04:56:04  PID[34788] Error      Uh oh, better call a programmer. This has gone s
ideways...
2013-05-13T04:56:08  PID[34788] Error      This is worse than you might think...
```

FIGURE 7-6

To detach from the live stream, press Ctrl+Break (or Ctrl+Pause, depending on your keyboard manufacturer) to cancel script execution and exit the console.

Downloading Logs via FTP

Capturing the live feed is great while you are connected, but sometimes you'll get a report that something went wrong when you weren't around to capture the details.

Well below the Quick Glance section on your website's dashboard is the link to the diagnostic log FTP endpoint. You can use your deployment credentials to access the FTP directory. Application trace logs are saved to the application folder of the diagnostic log FTP root (which points to the logFiles folder of the site's FTP root).

NOTE *Remember that when you enable application trace logging it is writing to the file system for your pool of websites. If you are in a free or shared scale mode, you have only 1GB of space across all your websites. Keep this in mind when you choose to enable trace output and the level of verbosity you wish to record, as all websites belonging to a pool that has hit its disk quota may become inaccessible until you resolve the space overage.*

SETTING UP AND USING CUSTOM DOMAINS

With tens or even dozens of people flocking to your site, you're going to want to get branding in place right away, and the allure of "yourwebsitetoendallwebsites.azurewebsites.net" isn't quite as squeaky clean as you would like. Once you have gone through the process of registering your domain, you'll of course want your traffic to be tied to your brand, and the next step is setting up custom domains for your Azure website. There are two pieces to this process; some configuration happens in the Azure portal and the rest occurs through the administrative interface provided by your DNS service.

NOTE *Remember that before you can customize the domain names to which your site responds, you must have moved your site up to a minimum scale setting of "shared."*

When you navigate to your website dashboard you can click the Configure tab to get to your domain settings. Provided you have set your website scaling mode to shared or reserved, you will be able to click the Manage Domains button to engage the dialog shown in Figure 7-7.

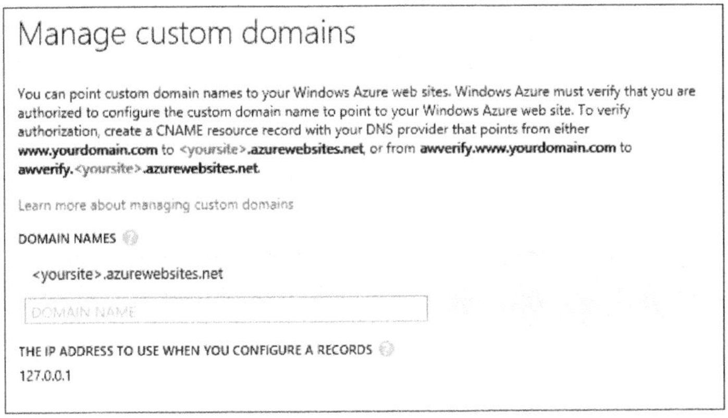

Manage custom domains

You can point custom domain names to your Windows Azure web sites. Windows Azure must verify that you are authorized to configure the custom domain name to point to your Windows Azure web site. To verify authorization, create a CNAME resource record with your DNS provider that points from either **www.yourdomain.com** to <yoursite>**.azurewebsites.net**, or from **awverify.www.yourdomain.com** to **awverify.**<yoursite>**.azurewebsites.net**.

Learn more about managing custom domains

DOMAIN NAMES

<yoursite>.azurewebsites.net

| DOMAIN NAME |

THE IP ADDRESS TO USE WHEN YOU CONFIGURE A RECORDS
127.0.0.1

FIGURE 7-7

This dialog spells out the items you'll need to check off your list in order to get a custom domain working. Essentially, that checklist proceeds like this:

1. Add a CNAME record to your domain's DNS host. This is the owner verification step and it needs to be completed before you can add your domain to Windows Azure Web Sites. Figure 7-7 provides some suggestions that you can use for your domain with the appropriate replacements. You'll also need to give the record some time to propagate so that the Windows Azure routers can resolve the DNS entry.

2. Add the domain to the website. You won't be able to complete this step until the verification CNAME has propagated out from your DNS server. Windows Azure will validate your domain for ownership before allowing you to associate a domain with your site.

3. Add an A record to your DNS host. While you can do this earlier — the IP address you need will be in the dialog shown in Figure 7-7 — Azure won't respond to requests until the preceding steps are complete. Also, if you have a live site, you won't want to make the change on your www host (or any wildcard) until Windows Azure has allowed you to associate the domain, so that you can avoid any service disruption.

Working with DNS providers varies considerably from host to host, so if you're not already familiar with your provider's administration system for managing CNAME and A records, you'll need to locate the appropriate documentation on their site.

WORKING WITH APPLICATION DEFAULTS

Developers have long used application settings in our web projects, simple key-value pairs that live in our web.config file and are often set specifically for a particular environment. You may already be using web.config transforms to target specific deployment targets, but the portal for Window Azure Web Sites gives you another option to set these values.

Note that values set in the portal for your application settings and connection strings will override anything that you have in your web.config file, even if you are using transforms. This is great for scenarios in which you share the source code to your website (such as open source) but don't want others to see values that may otherwise be sensitive to your deployment, such as usernames, passwords, or application keys for third-party services.

Working with Application Settings

Settings that you have created in your web.config file will not appear in the portal on their own. If you wish to set overrides, you need to add them to the "app settings" section on your Configure tab in all their key-value glory.

These settings are available to you through whichever language you are using on your site. In .NET, you can retrieve the values by key from the WebConfigurationManager.AppSettings collection.

```
WebConfigurationManager.AppSettings["MySetting"]
```

In PHP, you can use the getenv() command to extract the data:

```
getenv("MySetting")
```

Node.js has a slightly different convention, as app settings appear in dot notation format off of process.env:

```
process.env.MySetting
```

Remember that if you create or modify app settings in the portal, you need to click Save in the command bar to persist your values.

Setting Up Connection Strings

Connection strings fall into the same category as your application settings; and in the event that you can't make use of publishing profiles to set your connection strings, you can use the portal to set or override these values for your application. Figure 7-8 shows the simple three-field form required to add a connection string.

FIGURE 7-8

Like many other configuration settings in the portal, you need to click Save in the command bar to commit your changes.

> **NOTE** *If you are using Entity Framework (EF) Code First in your project and pass in a name to the base class constructor of your context, this is the name that you will want to use as the connection string name in your Windows Azure Web Site. By convention, EF first attempts to find a connection string of the same name you provide in that constructor, and this is by far the easiest way to wire up your SQL Database to EF in Windows Azure Web Sites. This is especially handy if you don't specify a connection string locally, electing instead to use the default convention for your local database.*

When you looked earlier at linking SQL Database resources in Chapter 6, you'll recall that by creating a link to the database the connection string was exposed in the Quick Glance section of your website's dashboard. You'll also recall that this does not implicitly make your application aware of the connection string, largely because you need a name associated with the value. You can, however, copy this connection string and paste it verbatim into the preceding form along with the appropriate name that would be expected by your application.

SETTING OTHER CONFIGURATION ELEMENTS

As you deploy your application you may need to set a few specific attributes of the site that are typically done once at initial deployment and then very rarely afterwards. You can access all these elements through the Configure tab of your site's dashboard. While these aren't the most exciting things you'll deal with when deploying or configuring your website, they can certainly be important should your site have specific technical requirements. This section will help you locate and control those pieces.

Setting Framework Versions

There are only two groups of options for this higher-level configuration element: your .NET version and the PHP version that you wish to run on your site, as shown in Figure 7-9. These are easy, push-button settings that can be committed to your site configuration by clicking Save in the command bar.

Talking about .NET Framework versions is one of the fastest ways to get your head spinning. For example, any version 2.0 will run on 3.0 and 3.5, both of which are based on, built from, and run on 2.0. Applications created under any of these versions are likely to run on 4.0, and therefore 4.5, which is binary compatible with 4.0.

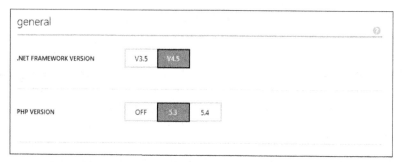

FIGURE 7-9

Of course, there can be some caveats and there are definitely some exceptions to the rule, so while the default is 4.5, you can choose to run 3.5 if your situation (or dependencies) requires it.

You'll likely turn off PHP if you don't need it for your site, but it doesn't do any harm to leave it on, as it's just a script/handler mapping and doesn't affect performance when your application is handled by a different run time, such as .NET.

There are some breaking changes between PHP 5.4 and 5.3, but you have the option to choose between the two as your needs prescribe; and if you need to support something outside of this range, the door is open for you to do so through custom handler mappings.

Adding Handler Mappings

Some folks run their own PHP build or have other modules that they would like to run in their WAWS application. You'll need to upload these native handlers via FTP to the bin directory of your site and create the mappings in the portal. Use the interface shown in Figure 7-10 to add any references you need and then click Save in the command bar.

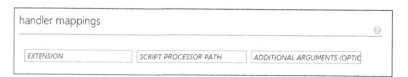

FIGURE 7-10

Keep in mind that when you specify the location of the handler, it has to be relative to the root path of your FTP directory.

NOTE *Managed handlers deployed in the bin directory of .NET applications can be config-ured instead through your* web.config *file. This gives you the added benefit of being able to configure and test application features while working in Visual Studio or through automated build and test servers and to keep a consistent approach to configuration throughout.*

Setting the Default Document

Default documents have almost gone the way of the dodo with the advent of friendly URLs and application-level routing, but a default document can still come in handy when your site is offline or for use as a landing page while you finalize your site. Another scenario is if you are building a static site from scratch or one of the many available templates on the web.

To modify the order or precedence or set which documents should be considered "default" for your website, navigate to the Configure tab in your website's dashboard. Default documents are near the bottom of the page. Use the interface shown in Figure 7-11 to add, remove, or sort documents.

default documents

default.aspx
index.php
hostingstart.html

DEFAULT DOCUMENT

FIGURE 7-11

Note that in the absence of the first document in your list the web server will attempt to locate the second document, and so on. The server will work through the list to resolve any request without a document name in the URL to a directory on your server. This gives you flexibility regarding how you name your documents across your website.

SUMMARY

Windows Azure Web Sites enables you to start small and scale up as you need, from capacity and storage space to processing power and handling increased request volume on your site. If you plan to double your traffic every day, Windows Azure should be able to keep up with your growth for at least the first few exponents without much trouble at all.

As you push your application to the cloud you are now equipped to modify its configuration on the fly, keep your sensitive data private, and even track down errors more easily with a number of different tools and approaches. In addition, by combining some of this information with other concepts covered earlier in the book, you should also be able to formulate how these capabilities can help you out in automation scenarios.

Finally, if you find that you're missing a critical component in the features of your Windows Azure Web Site, you'll now be able to select other options or even extend the included functionality by incorporating additional functionality and configuration as required.

8 Deploying and Configuring a Cloud Application

IN THIS CHAPTER:

> ➤ A walk-through of the project's core assets

> ➤ Background technical information on how the application is implemented and operates

> ➤ Examples of deployment to and configuration of a site in the cloud

WROX.COM CODE DOWNLOADS FOR THIS CHAPTER

You need to download the MovieFu.zip file.

While the goal of this book centers primarily on deploying and maintaining websites in Windows Azure, it would be hard to get a full picture of the process and its nuances without a concrete example from which to work. You can read all you want to about how to ride a horse, but it's a whole different story when you finally get on the saddle! For that reason, you're about to saddle up and walk through the deployment and configuration of an actual reference application. This will enable you to learn about the various aspects of the deployment process as well as manage your deployments once they are out in the cloud.

EXPLORING THE MOVIEFU APPLICATION

So here's the premise: Imagine you have a great collection of movies that you want to track and share with your friends. You even want to give them a chance to comment on the movies and rate them, which is great information to have if you decide to host a movie night. You set up a website that enables you to create your library of flicks, search for movies, and keep track of the directors that make your favorite films. You call the site MovieFu and build the application using the ASP.NET MVC Framework.

Again, this book — and even this chapter — is not about teaching you how to build websites on ASP.NET or helping you learn the MVC Framework. There are many good references out there for that. This project is not the pinnacle of code quality, it's not the best-looking date at the UI design ball, nor is it meant to represent best practices, but it does illustrate the kinds of things you may be doing when you publish to WAWS.

Deploying and Running the Application Locally

The first thing you need to do is get the code for the app so that you can start exploring it. If you have met the requirements described in the What You Need to Use This Book section of the Introduction, it is ready to go and will run for you out of the box.

Downloading the Code

You can find the code for this chapter at Wrox.com. The instructions for locating the code and downloading it are located in the Introduction to this book. The code itself is in a zip file. Once downloaded, right-click on the file in File Explorer and select the Properties option in the context menu. In the Properties dialog, on the General tab, there is a section labeled Security. For files that have been downloaded from the Internet, this section includes an Unblock button. If you see this button, click it, and then click OK. This is not a requirement, but it eliminates some annoying warning messages when you open the project in Visual Studio.

Now that you have the code in a zip file, extract it (by right-clicking on the file and selecting Extract All, or using any other method of your choosing) to a directory.

Launching the Application

Take a few minutes to launch the application and ensure that your machine is correctly configured and that you have all the files you need to get started:

1. Locate the directory where you saved the project files.

2. Navigate to the MovieFu folder where the solution file is located.

3. Double-click the MovieFu.sln file to launch Visual Studio.

4. Right-click on the solution in Solution Explorer and click Enable NuGet Package Restore.

NOTE *If you have multiple versions of Visual Studio installed on your machine you may be prompted to select the version in which to load the solution. If you're presented with this choice, be sure to pick Visual Studio 2012 to take advantage of the features related to publishing your application to Windows Azure.*

---

5. Press Ctrl+F5 to run the application, or select Debug ➪ Start Without Debugging to launch the application. The window shown in Figure 8-1 should appear when your application is running.

That's it! You can close the browser window at this point and return to Visual Studio. You'll examine the application later in this chapter, but first you're going to look at the bits that make the website tick.

FIGURE 8-1

Examining Application Components

There aren't too many surprises in MovieFu, and you can expect to find most of the resources where they would be in any MVC 4 application. The website was created as an ASP.NET MVC 4 Web Application project, using the Empty Application template. The Twitter.Bootstrap.Mvc4 open-source library adds some style to the website and gives you tools, such as automatic scaffolding of standard CRUD views.

You should familiarize yourself with the following major elements to become comfortable working with the application:

➤ **Controllers, models, and views** — All of these components are located in their default location and follow the MVC Framework convention. All controllers, for example, are located in the Controllers folder. Similarly, views can be found in the View folder in subdirectories named after the controller to which they are associated.

➤ **Membership and authentication** — Membership is provided through the ASP .NET MVC 4 Web Application project template and implemented through the SimpleMembership provider. This is a basic kick-start that enables wiring to third-party authentication providers, if you choose. In MovieFu, this default implementation has been modified to share a database context with the main site data. Important classes to examine would be Configuration.cs and the Initial Run migration, both located in the Migrations folder.

➤ **Authorization** — Any membership provider built on top of the ASP.NET membership system, SimpleMembership included, allows you to use out-of-the-box functionality for authorization. Have a look at the MovieController.cs class to see how authorization can be implemented by decorating the controller with an Authorize attribute.

➤ **Repositories** — MovieFu employs the Inversion of Control (IoC) library Ninject to provide constructor injection on the controller classes (this is also known as dependency injection, or DI). The Repositories folder contains the interfaces you need to access the database using the Repository pattern and simple implementations of those interfaces.

➤ **The Site Layout** — Later in this chapter you'll work with some configuration options through the Management Portal. This allows you to dynamically set the text displayed as the website's title. Have a look in the `_BootstrapLayout.basic.cshtml` file to locate the application setting that you'll be targeting.

Creating the Database with Entity Framework

Those of you who are experienced in ASP.NET know that you're not locked into any specific database platform. This is one of the best things about using a mature framework; you have not only the freedom to choose which database back end to leverage, but also the flexibility to do so when required. It can be very frustrating to work inside a technology stack that demands specific requirements and doesn't easily allow you to satisfy your project's functional requirements. This is especially true in integration projects or extensions to legacy systems when you aren't given the option to elect which back end you'll be building from or adding to. Whether it is MS SQL, Oracle, MySQL, or a no-SQL solution that you'll be using to maintain your application's data, ASP.NET likely has the providers for you to connect and manipulate data. As a greenfield project, MovieFu is not bound by many constraints and could have used any number of solutions.

That said, the tools that Microsoft provides to developers are typically aligned with the technology stack for which they are actively developing and providing guidance. Visual Studio has some great tooling and support for MVC and Entity Framework acting in unison, and Entity Framework is currently the data access technology that is recommended by Microsoft for anyone starting a new project. For these reasons, MovieFu was built to dynamically generate the database using Entity Framework Code First.

NOTE *Entity Framework is an object-relational mapper (ORM) that handles most of the details related to connecting to the database as well as managing entity state and persistence. Entity Framework enables you to define the model in a number of ways. A common approach for applications for which there is already a database involves using the database schema to generate the initial model. Customizations can be executed afterwards, but the entities tend to be very close to the database table structure.*

A second approach that recent versions of Entity Framework support is known as Code First. You start by creating a number of different classes, each with its own collection of properties. Then a database schema can be generated based on the properties in each class.

The default templates for many web projects in Visual Studio 2012 now include Entity Framework by default — which you can verify in the `Packages.Config` file in the root of your project — but you can also add it to any application or library by installing it through the Package Manager Console, shown in Figure 8-2.

Alternatively, you can add Entity Framework through the Manage NuGet Packages dialog, shown in Figure 8-3.

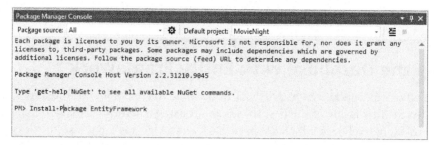

FIGURE 8-2

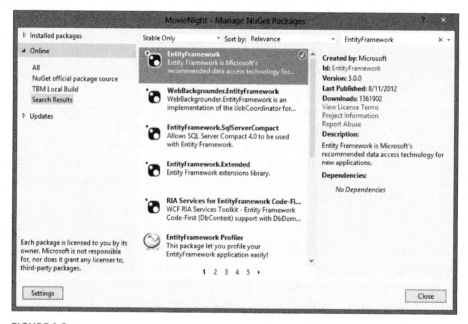

FIGURE 8-3

Understanding Entity Framework

As a block of code, Entity Framework is two important things. First, it's an open-source project that anyone is free to contribute to and work with. This means you can go to the project website, clone the source code, make changes, and then submit pull requests. Second, it's a versioned, signed library that is considered a supported product by Microsoft, which means you are allowed to use it in your projects as you would any other code provided by Microsoft, released under the Apache License 2.0.

As a library that you will use in your application, Entity Framework allows you to work with default settings to connect to a database and provides you with extra tools to manage entities. It includes Visual Studio designers that enable you to work with existing databases or start from scratch, and beginning with version 4.3 it is possible to use plain old CLR objects (POCOs) to lay out your data model with the support of migrations. This is the Code First strategy described earlier.

Reviewing the Basics of Entity Framework Code First

Thanks to Code First, you can start by writing a simple POCO to represent your entity, such as the Movie class in Listing 8-1, just as you would in any other project.

LISTING 8-1

```
public class Movie
{
    public int MovieId { get; set; }
    public string Title { get; set; }
    public string Description { get; set; }
    public string ImageUrl { get; set; }
}
```

This model is just a class with primitive types as properties to describe a movie that you will store in the application. However, this class serves as a base that you can augment, decorate, and effectively define advanced schema attributes for what will become a table in a database and how the model will be validated. Listing 8-2 starts to illustrate how a POCO can incorporate some of those features, including marking fields as required. In the case of ReleaseYear, the Range attribute provides framework-level validation instructions that can be used from JavaScript libraries or in your controller. Virtual members enable you to create references to other tables and more easily access related data, using a pattern known as Lazy Loading; these members are also known as Navigation Properties.

LISTING 8-2

```
public class Movie
{
    public Movie()
    {
        this.ReleaseYear = DateTime.Now.Year;
        this.Ratings = new HashSet<Rating>();
    }

    public int Id { get; set; }

    [Required]
    public string Title { get; set; }
    [Required]
    public string Description { get; set; }
    [Range(1877,2020)]
```

LISTING 8-2 *(Continued)*

```
public int ReleaseYear { get; set; }

public virtual int DirectorId { get; set; }
public virtual Person Director { get; set; }

public ICollection<Rating> Ratings { get; set; }
}
```

By itself, the Movie class is nothing more than a blueprint of an object that you can instantiate, but when you add the DbContext in Listing 8-3 to your application, you can start to think of that movie as a row in a database.

LISTING 8-3

```
public class MovieFuContext :DbContext
{
    public DbSet<Movie> Movies { get; set; }
}
```

When you create an instance of a MovieFuContext object, Entity Framework uses a series of conventions to attempt to make a database connection. Failing this connection through a series of strategies, Code First kicks in, using a default configuration to create the database on your behalf and subsequently issuing the commands required to create your tables. At this point, it is impossible to provide specific details regarding what these defaults will be for you, as it depends on the version mix of Entity Framework and Visual Studio that you are using; however, looking in web.config will tell you how Entity Framework wired itself up, as shown in Listing 8-4 from the web.config in MovieFu. In this case, the sample application was created with Visual Studio 2012, and Entity Framework 5.0 is using Local Db.

LISTING 8-4

```
<defaultConnectionFactory type="System.Data.Entity.Infrastructure
.LocalDbConnectionFactory, EntityFramework">
   <parameters>
     <parameter value="v11.0" />
   </parameters>
</defaultConnectionFactory>
```

Enabling Migrations

At this point, you have created a solid solution: low overhead to create tables and the database itself; default conventions for accessing the database; and the capability to override the defaults to meet your needs. But what happens when you need to add fields to a table, or add new tables? This is where migrations enter the picture, enabling you to control how changes are applied in the database, modify existing table structures, and seed data — and because these actions are all expressed through code, you can do some crafty things and handle these processes differently depending on where the code is executing.

While migrations are enabled in the solution you're working through, they are not enabled by default. If you need to enable them in a project, follow these steps:

1. Open the Package Manager Console, accessible through View ➪ Other Windows ➪ Package Manager Console.

2. Select the project you wish to target from the dropdown menu.

3. In the console type the following command: `Enable-Migrations`.

This will create a `Configuration.cs` file in your application with a class called `Configuration` that inherits from a generic class named `DbMigrationsConfiguration`. The inheritance specifies the `DbContext` that you have in your project, and a constructor is created for you by default that disables automatic migrations (this is a good thing!). Only one (useful) override is available: `Seed`, which enables you to manipulate the database anytime a migration is applied. Listing 8-5, the `Configuration` class for MovieFu, demonstrates one way to ensure that a base set of data is available in your application through the `AddOrUpdate` method. `AddOrUpdate` works by specifying how you want to identify a seed value — MovieFu uses the name of `Theme` — and what value you want to either ensure is in there or adjust. While `Theme` is a fairly simple object, imagine more complex objects whose required initial values change throughout a project's development.

LISTING 8-5

```
internal sealed class Configuration : DbMigrationsConfiguration<MovieFu.Models
.MovieFuContext>
{
    public Configuration()
    {
        AutomaticMigrationsEnabled = false;
    }

    protected override void Seed(MovieFu.Models.MovieFuContext context)
    {
        context.Themes.AddOrUpdate(t => t.Name,
            new Theme { Name = "Favorite Superhero" },
            new Theme { Name = "Retro 80's" },
            new Theme { Name = "Disco Nights" },
            new Theme { Name = "Wild, Wild West" },
            new Theme { Name = "Favorite Character From the Movie" },
            new Theme { Name = "Famous Dead People" },
```

LISTING 8-5 *(Continued)*

```
        new Theme { Name = "PJ Party" },
        new Theme { Name = "Boring old Plain Clothes" }
        );

    }

}
```

NOTE *Automatic migrations are a groovy but not always practical addition to your tool-box. They enable you to easily update the database without having code files that provide explicit instructions on how to do it. Unfortunately, the luxury is not without its costs: You can't "downgrade" your database, you don't get named versions of your database, and there are a number of things they can't do for you, such as properly rename columns; therefore, they should only be used in experimental scenarios. I don't recommend using them in any code that is destined for a production environment, but they can be a great way to explore Entity Framework.*

Adding Migrations to Your Project

With migrations enabled, you can now start to look at the code that drives the changes. Each migration is a class that inherits from DbMigration, giving you a rich set of operations to perform on the database. To see a complete list, visit http://msdn.microsoft.com/en-us/library/system.data.entity.migrations.dbmigration(v=vs.103).aspx.

Migrations can be as simple as renaming a field. For example, consider the code in Listing 8-6, which renames the MovieTitle column to Title in a table called Movies.

LISTING 8-6

```
public class SampleMigration : DbMigration
{
    public override void Up()
    {
        RenameColumn("dbo.Movies", "MovieTitle", "Title");
    }
}
```

The Up() method is abstract in the base class and thus the only member that you need to implement. There is also a virtual method called Down(), illustrated in Listing 8-7, that you can elect to override, which enables you to change the name of the column back to its original name.

LISTING 8-7

```
public override void Down()
{
    RenameColumn("dbo.Movies", "Title", "MovieTitle");
}
```

Why might you want to do this? When you ask Entity Framework to move your database to a specific version, all the explicit migrations from the current version to the target version are discovered in your project through reflection and then executed. If you are moving to a higher version, the Up() method is called on each migration in order until the target version is reached. Likewise, if you are moving to a lower version, the Down() method is called, if it exists, until Entity Framework lands on the version you requested. In addition, if you follow the practice of tying your product releases to a database version, you'll have code that targets a different data structure, which is precisely why you should implement the Down method in your migrations. When you start the app after a downward migration and the code executes, it will try to create classes, invoke actions, and render views; and it will expect entities to be consistent with the version in question.

After you have enabled migrations, you need to create one anytime a field or table change is required. Thankfully, there is a whole set of tooling to help build this out on your behalf.

You create a migration by returning to the Package Manager Console and executing the Add-Migration command, passing the name of your migration as a parameter: Add-Migration Your-Migration-Name.

As a best practice, give the migration a meaningful name that lets other developers (and you, in the future) know what purpose it serves. The example in Listing 8-8 shows the migration I created when adding an ImageUrl property to the Movie class.

LISTING 8-8

```
public partial class movieimage : DbMigration
{
    public override void Up()
    {
        AddColumn("dbo.Movies", "ImageUrl", c => c.String());
    }

    public override void Down()
    {
        DropColumn("dbo.Movies", "ImageUrl");
    }
}
```

Finding Migrations and Related Files

All the migrations, as well as the configuration class, are located in the Migrations folder in the root of your project. This is a convention that is followed by the tooling in Entity Framework, and each new generated class will appear in the same directory.

The last thing you'll need to know is how Entity Framework is signaled from MovieFu in order to start migrations. MovieFu employs a very basic strategy for the purpose of this book: Migrate to the latest version of the database when the application is launched. You will find the following line of code in Global.asax.cs:

```
Database.SetInitializer(
    new MigrateDatabaseToLatestVersion<MovieFu.Models.MovieFuContext,
    Migrations.Configuration>()
);
```

This tells Entity Framework to move to the latest version of the MovieFuContext using the configuration from the specified class.

FAMILIARIZING YOURSELF WITH THE APPLICATION

You had a quick look at the site earlier in the chapter, but now it is time to explore some of the available functionality more deeply. The site requires a little bit of data entry to be somewhat useful, and you'll need to be signed in to do any data editing.

Registering to Use the Site

The People and Movies links resolve to actions on controllers that are protected by an Authorize attribute. If you try to access them you'll be redirected to a login page where you can use existing credentials or click through to the Register page, which is shown in Figure 8-4.

When you deploy the site none of the users you create will move to the cloud with the site. Because you're using Code First and EF, a new database will be created in Winodws Azure SQL Database as the code is executed on the live site.

Creating Movies and People

You can access the create screens for both Movies and People from the website's menu at the top of the screen. Movies have a Director property that needs to be set by selecting someone from the People table, as shown in Figure 8-5.

To help facilitate this, a few features have been put in place to kick-start the data entry process. First, the open-source library AngelaSmith is used in the Seed method of the migrations Configuration class to generate a random list of 15 people. Next, the same method does a quick count of the movies in the database, and if none are present it proceeds to populate it with a few titles.

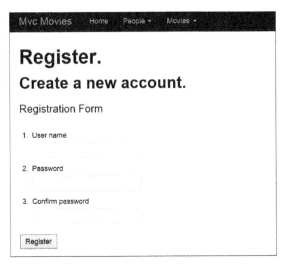

FIGURE 8-4

FIGURE 8-5

Adding Ratings

With a few movies in place you can now start telling your friends about the site and inviting them to sign up, sign in, and start rating your library. The form to add a rating is shown in Figure 8-6 and can be located on the Details view of any movie on the site.

FIGURE 8-6

As folks add movie ratings, they will appear on the movie's detail page above the rating form.

DEPLOYING AND CONFIGURING MOVIEFU

It's time for the big show! You're ready to push that site out into the wild and bring it to life, and you have the instructions from this book to guide you. If you would like to take a stab at it on your own, here are the steps you need to do to get it live:

1. Create a new website and corresponding Windows Azure SQL Database in the Management Portal and download the publish profile.

2. Import the profile to your project and publish the site.

3. Override the application name stored in the web.config file by introducing application settings in the Management Portal and name it something you prefer.

The following sections provide the complete instructions.

Creating a Site and Database

For explanations and screenshots along the way, you can review Chapters 1 and 2, which go into greater detail. To follow along more quickly if you're comfortable with the process, log into the Management Portal and navigate to the Web Sites listing, then follow these steps:

1. Create a new website by selecting New ➪ Compute ➪ Web Site ➪ Custom Create.

2. Choose a name for your site, elect to create a new database, and set the name of the connection string to **MovieFuConnection**. Then click Next.

3. Choose to create a new database server. Enter credentials that you'll be able to remember, then click OK to create your website and database.

4. Navigate to the website's dashboard to download the publish profile and save it in a location you'll be able to locate in the next section.

Publishing the Site

Chapters 2 and 4 cover various aspects of publishing and configuring the site, including downloading profiles and incorporating your Azure settings into your tools. To follow along here, make sure you have the solution opened in Visual Studio 2012, and then perform these steps:

1. Click Build ⇨ Publish MovieFu.

2. Click Import and select the publish profile that you previously downloaded, browse to the file, select it, then click OK. Note that, as shown in Figure 8-7, you have the option to also add your Windows Azure subscription, which would allow you to directly target a site to publish to.

3. Review the connection information, then click Next.

4. Select the connection string from the dropdown to replace the MovieFuConnection connection string as part of the deployment process. Be sure to check the option to update the destination web.config file.

5. Click Next, then Publish.

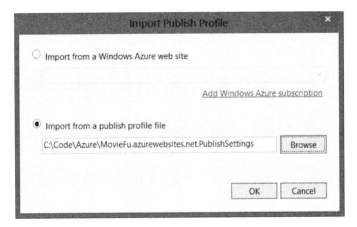

FIGURE 8-7

Visual Studio 2012 will compile the list of files that need to move to the cloud, create a deployment script, and push everything you need up to your website. Your browser will open and in a few moments your site will be displayed.

Changing Application Settings

You can override the settings of the application in a number of different ways as illustrated in Chapters 4 and 7. Here, you'll use the Management Portal to override the name of the application that is displayed in the website's menu:

1. Navigate to the website's dashboard in the Management Portal and click the Configure tab.

2. Scroll down to the App Settings section.

3. Add a new application setting with a key called "ApplicationName" (without quotes) and choose a name for your site. Put the name in the Value field.

4. Press Save on the command bar at the bottom of the portal.

As soon as the portal is done saving the configuration of your site, you can press the Browse button on the command bar to see the changes. Your application name will be updated in the menu.

Refining Your Skills

You've been skinning cats all different kinds of ways throughout the book, so why not try your hand at some additional exercises that will help develop your skills?

➤ Use PowerShell to change the name of the site as it's displayed by adding or modifying the appropriate key/value pair.

➤ Rather than deploy the site through Visual Studio, commit your site to a source control repository and configure the website to use deployments.

➤ Experiment with Visual Studio's integration with Windows Azure Web Sites through Server Explorer to manage your application state or monitor site logs as they are written.

➤ Explore other options that Azure has to offer, such as the use of a Storage account to host your static assets and reduce IIS processing load. Media that you have on your site, such as audio, video, or images, as well as static source files for scripts or CSS, are excellent candidates for storage and could save you money on egress traffic.

SUMMARY

Most folks feel better equipped to learn a new technology when they can start to work from a place they are already familiar with. Throughout this chapter you explored an ASP.NET MVC website that demonstrates qualities of applications you may already be working on and will be able to adapt to cloud deployment.

You examined the key components of the application and considered aspects such as membership, authorization, and database migrations. With MovieFu, a working application with a lot of room to grow, you can continue to learn, push, poke, prod, and extend an application that runs in the cloud. Congrats!

INDEX

CPSIA information can be obtained
at www.ICGtesting.com
Printed in the USA
PW09s1717061217
10BV00025B/1365/P

9 781118 678527